Gender, Bullying, and Harassment

Gender, Bullying, and Harassment

Strategies to End Sexism and Homophobia in Schools

Elizabeth J. Meyer

FOREWORD BY
LYN MIKEL BROWN

Teachers College
Columbia University
New York and London

Published by Teachers College Press, 1234 Amsterdam Avenue, New York, NY 10027

Library of Congress Cataloging-in-Publication Data

Meyer, Elizabeth J.
  Gender, bullying, and harassment : strategies to end sexism and homophobia in schools / Elizabeth J. Meyer.
     p. cm.
  Includes bibliographical references and index.
  ISBN 978-0-8077-4953-1 (pbk. : alk. paper) — ISBN 978-0-8077-4954-8 (hardcover : alk. paper) 1. Homophobia in schools--United States. 2. Sexism in education—United States. 3. Bullying in schools—United States. 4. School violence—United States. I. Title.
  LC212.82.M49 2009
  371.826'64--dc22

                                                                                    2008055598

ISBN 978-0-8077-4953-1 (paperback)
ISBN 978-0-8077-4954-8 (hardcover)

Printed on acid-free paper

Manufactured in the United States of America

16 15 14 13 12 11 10 09   8 7 6 5 4 3 2 1

Contents

Foreword

I found out about the topic of this book through the back door, so to speak. I had been researching relationships between girls, which led me to their friendships, which led me to a study of girlfighting behavior. After analyzing over 400 interviews and focus groups, and with 20 years of listening to, teaching about, and working with girls, I felt I had a pretty good grasp of the reasons why girls betray and hurt one another and how schools can interrupt or unwittingly encourage their behavior. Soon after I finished this research, I was invited to participate in a statewide task force on school climate.

The task force was mostly made up of bully-prevention experts and me. I was struck immediately by the lack of meaningful connection between what I had learned from girls and the literature provided, most of which described bullying within only one paradigm. Bullies were portrayed as impulsive, impudent rule-breakers, who lack compassion, have a strong drive to dominate, and act aggressively toward adults. The girls in my study, on the other hand, thought about their behavior, often expressed regret afterwards, and struggled with their desire for power. Many of them followed the rules and policed the boundaries of gender conformity; adults tended to like them because they appeared civilized and nice. Bullies were also said to be motivated by a strong need for dominance, a hostile attitude to their surroundings, and a need for material and psychological rewards. The girls in my study, however, were often motivated by underlying frustration with unfair treatment and harassment in school, the pressure they felt to match up to media ideals of beauty and perfection, and the promise of visibility and attention from boys. How could a program purported to be a "universal intervention for the reduction and prevention of bully/victim problems" speak so little to issues relevant to girls' aggression?

Not surprising, then, my work with this task force was fraught. I soon discovered that not considering the role of gender is endemic to bully prevention approaches. In meetings I experienced what it felt like to be the problem, the one who "didn't get it," who interrupted the flow of progress.

My colleagues were good, smart people who listened patiently, but they remained convinced that every assumption I questioned and every absence I noted could be explained away or subsumed under a bully-prevention model.

I started to think that maybe "bully prevention" had become a bit of a bully itself, threatening to push aside the richly diverse reality of children's lives for one-size-fits-all trainings, discipline charts, and consistent consequences. If the "bullying" was to generically stand in for sexism, racism, homophobia, sexual harassment, and even hate crimes, how could we affirm students' different experiences not only with one another but also in relation to the rules and structure of their schools? If we don't help students name these differences, how can we educate them about their rights and encourage complex and meaningful solutions to their problems?

I wished I had had this smart, brave book as I struggled to articulate these and other questions. Elizabeth Meyer speaks clearly and sensibly about differences that make a difference in children's school lives. She distinguishes bullying from various forms of gendered harassment and connects psychological and relational power struggles to the systemic and structural problems that can fuel them. She identifies existing legal protections, such as Title IX, lest we unwittingly undermine them with bully prevention policies that sound inclusive but in reality exclude many, that sound powerful but in practice undermine students' rights. At a time when bully prevention has all but taken over the social realities of schools, Elizabeth Meyer encourages us to reconsider our assumptions and challenge what is taken for granted. She reminds us that the best way to ensure student safety is to offer children what we ourselves would want—someone willing to set aside simple categories and look beyond the surface of things, someone who will listen carefully and take us seriously.

Lyn Mikel Brown

Preface

On February 12, 2008, 15-year-old Larry King was shot in the computer classroom of his California junior high school by another male student after Larry had asked him to be his valentine. Larry was known in his school not only for being openly gay but also for wearing high heels, nail polish, and makeup. This tragic incident is one of the more recent and extreme examples of why it was important to write this book. Educators, parents, and youth need more information and resources about how to address forms of bullying and harassment that are influenced by gender. Gender is an important force in shaping behaviors and informs how we interact with each other and understand ourselves. Unfortunately, the role that gender plays in many incidents of bullying and harassment is often overlooked or accepted as normal, which allows the problem to persist. This book intends to change this trend by providing a new lens for understanding bullying and harassment as well as strategies for ending these phenomena in schools.

As a former high school teacher, I remember how helpless I felt to assist students who turned to me for support in the face of harassment. During my first year of teaching, I had one student come to me on a regular basis to confide in me about all of the taunts and harassment she was enduring. I could see the impact it was having on her health and academic performance, but I didn't know how to help. I offered her individual support but couldn't get other teachers or the administration to address it in a systematic or meaningful way. Everyone seemed to accept sexual harassment and homophobic insults as part of the school culture, and my efforts to work against them were met with extreme resistance and inertia.

In my second teaching job, things weren't much better. Gay students were stalked and made fun of, female students were sexually harassed by male peers, and words like *fag*, *bitch*, and *dyke* were commonly used by students to insult and mock their peers. Few of my colleagues or administrators were willing to take clear steps to stop these behaviors. Although I made attempts to engage colleagues in dialogue, worked with the administration to raise their awareness, and attended workshops to expand my understanding

of the problem, none of it seemed to have an impact. I was just one classroom teacher, not an "expert" on the issue. The head of the school told me
he would need more time and information before he took any specific actions to address the problem.

After teaching in high school classrooms for 5 years, I was frustrated
with the institutional inaction on these issues and decided to return to
graduate school to learn how to help schools address these issues more
proactively. I had to become the expert they were looking for in order
to help address the problem. I taught in the United States and studied in
Canada, interviewed teachers in both countries, and have worked in classrooms and with community groups in both countries and have found that
the issues in schools in terms of trying to reduce gendered harassment in
the United States and Canada are quite similar in spite of their very different legal protections.

INTRODUCTION TO THE PROBLEM

Recent research shows that bullying and harassment are common and
prevalent behaviors in secondary schools. In the first study to look at both
bullying and sexual harassment simultaneously, researchers found that ap-
proximately 52% of students have been bullied at school and 35% have
been sexually harassed (Gruber & Fineran, 2008). This study also found
that students who identified as gay, lesbian, bisexual, or questioning their
sexual orientation experienced more bullying (79%) and sexual harassment
(71%) than other students (Gruber & Fineran, 2008). Finally, Gruber and
Fineran concluded that although sexual harassment was less frequent than
bullying, it had greater impacts on health factors such as self-esteem, mental health, physical health, trauma symptoms, and substance abuse (Gruber
& Fineran, 2008). This study is important because it points to the need to
address the issues of bullying and harassment separately so that important
resources and training time can be allocated to adequately prepare educators to understand and respond appropriately to these different harmful behaviors. As the literature review in Chapter 2 will demonstrate, most
bullying studies and intervention programs do not explicitly address issues
related to gender and sexual orientation, which often allows these forms of
harassment to persist.

There have also been several recent legal cases where students have successfully taken action against their schools for not responding appropriately
in severe cases of sexual and homophobic harassment as well as harassment for gender nonconformity. One such case is *Theno v. Tonganoxie Unified School District* (2005). In this case, a male student, Dylan Theno, was

subjected to persistent and severe verbal harassment that included comments about masturbation, oral sex, and anti-gay slurs such as *fag.* In this case the court found that "the plaintiff was harassed because he failed to satisfy his peers' stereotyped expectations for his gender because the primary objective of plaintiff's harassers appears to have been to disparage his perceived lack of masculinity" *(Theno v. Tonganoxie Unified School District,* 2005, p. 11). The harassment was found to be so extreme that it denied him access to education, and the school district settled for $440,000 (Trowbridge, 2005). The high price tag associated with this case and others like it sends a message to school districts that they need to be more proactive in how they address such incidents in their schools.

RESEARCH METHODS

The research in this book was conducted from 2003 to 2008 and includes interview data from teachers in the United States and Canada who agreed to participate in this study. The author conducted in-depth interviews with eight teachers working in secondary schools in two public school districts (Patton, 2002; Van Manen, 1997). Participants were recruited using both maximum variation and snowball sampling methods (Maykut & Morehouse, 1994) to ensure that a broad range of experiences and perspectives were included. Maximum variation sampling, also known as purposive sampling, seeks out persons who represent the most diverse range of experiences with a phenomenon (Lincoln & Guba, 1985; Maykut & Morehouse, 1994). Snowball sampling was also useful in this study, since it helped address the problems of access to participants. This form of sampling starts with one or two key informants, who then refer colleagues to participate in this project. This word-of-mouth recruitment ensured that participants were more personally invested in the research and met the objectives of locating teachers from a diverse range of backgrounds and professional experience. In order to protect their identities, they will not be profiled individually with their demographic information. Instead, the numbers of teachers who self-identified with each given descriptive category are presented in Figure P.1

Through a series of three open-ended interviews (Seidman, 1998), teachers described how they perceived and responded to incidences of bullying, racial harassment, sexual harassment, homophobic harassment, and harassment for gender nonconformity in the context of their individual experiences in their schools' cultures. The first interview focused on the teacher's career path, philosophy, and roles in the classroom and then discussed the general issue of bullying. The concept of biased harassment was introduced in this first interview by discussing issues of race and ethnicity and related

Figure P.1. Participant Demographics (*N* = 8)

Gender	Religion
5 men	4 No affiliation
3 women	1 Christian
	1 Muslim
Sexual Orientation	1 Bahai
5 heterosexual	1 Unitarian/Pagan
3 gay or bisexual	
	Years Teaching
Ethnicity	1–5 years: 3
5 Euro-Canadian/Euro-American	5–10 years: 3
1 Indian	10+ years: 2
1 French-Canadian/Métis	Average: 11.2
1 Arab	
	Citizenship
Languages	4–1st generation Canadian/U.S. citizen
1st (Native)	3–5th+ generation Canadian/U.S. citizen
6 English	1–2nd generation Canadian/U.S. citizen
1 French	
1 Hindi	**Age**
2nd (Fluent)	Min: 27
3 French	Max: 51
2 English	Average: 35
1 Arabic	

forms of harassment in their schools. The second interview focused on the three types of gendered harassment that are the focus of this book: sexual harassment, sexual orientation harassment, and harassment for gender nonconformity. The third interview allowed teachers to reflect on the discussions of the first two and draw connections and explore their (in)actions in their current school contexts. These interviews were tape-recorded and transcribed for analysis. Data analysis was conducted in an ongoing and exploratory design as this research sought to uncover common themes between teachers' experiences to help inform future studies and school interventions (Maykut & Morehouse, 1994). The data were analyzed using both contextual and thematic codes that situated the teachers' identities and experiences within their school contexts and allowed common themes to emerge among their experiences.

In addition to interview data, policy documents were collected from the ministry, school board, and school level. A content analysis of these

documents was conducted to identify references to bullying, racial or ethnic harassment, sexual harassment, sexual orientation harassment, and harassment for gender nonconformity. This content was then compared with
teacher interview data to identify the relationships between official school
policies and reported teacher practice. The school-level documents that
were included in this phase of the study were teachers' handbooks, student
agendas, school mission statements, and codes of conduct. These documents
were located on official school and school board Web sites and provided by
the teachers during the interview process.

Each of these documents was read and analyzed for any discussion of
bullying and harassment. Particular attention was paid to definitions of
these terms and whether they explicitly named any of the following: race,
ethnicity, sexual orientation, sexual harassment, and/or gender identity and
expression. They were also examined to see if they included response protocols and, if so, how they differed for various infractions. These artifacts
were also consulted during the analysis of the teacher interview data to
determine the level of teachers' knowledge about their own schools' policies
and the extent to which they felt they had been informed about such policies
and to determine whether these official documents impacted their reports of
their own classroom practice.

STRUCTURE OF THE BOOK

The goal of this book is to provide education professionals, family members, community groups, and other youth workers with an accessible source
of information on how to understand and take action to correct the problems related to gender, bullying, and harassment in schools. Chapter 1 presents an overview of the main forms of harassment addressed in this book:
sexual orientation harassment, sexual harassment, and harassment for gender nonconformity. These three forms of harassment are combined under a
new term: gendered harassment. This term makes explicit the common link
behind all of these behaviors, which is the policing of the boundaries of traditional heterosexual gender roles. These boundaries are constructed within
a society that privileges certain relationships, gender identities, and sexual
orientations over others.

Chapter 2 is a summary and analysis of the research that has been conducted on bullying and harassment. This chapter is an important one for
stakeholders to read in order to understand why current bullying interventions have been structured the way they have and why most anti-bullying
initiatives will not be effective at combating forms of gendered harassment.
This also provides the context for the rest of the book and will offer the

reader an introduction to what we know about bullying and harassment in schools and what information is still missing.

Chapter 3 presents information about school culture that emerged from interviews with teachers and the research literature. This chapter discusses the formal and informal influences that shape what goes on in schools and how the school culture has a significant impact on what teachers feel they can and can't do to take a stand against gendered harassment. Understanding how school cultures work is an essential first step to creating effective responses to bullying and harassment.

Chapter 4 addresses the problem of bullying and harassment from teachers' perspectives. The rich data that emerged from talking with teachers about the challenges they face in schools can provide education professionals and concerned community members with important information about what barriers exist for teachers trying to reduce bullying and harassment. Teachers have the most direct contact with students and are the ones who are expected to address most forms of bullying and harassment in schools. Therefore, it is important to understand the variables that influence why teachers choose to intervene in certain situations but not others. The professional experiences of these teachers as well as their personal identities offer valuable insights into the many layers that schools must address if they are to effectively reduce these negative behaviors.

Chapter 5 is an overview of key legal decisions related to forms of gendered harassment in schools. It is written in a case study format to help the layperson understand the legal expectations placed upon schools when dealing with forms of harassment. It describes seven different cases of students who sued their schools for failing to protect them from forms of gendered harassment and their outcomes. The chapter concludes with a summary of specific actions schools can take to protect their students from harm and themselves from liability.

Finally, Chapter 6 provides a summary of the key points made in the book, as well as specific recommendations for change in schools. In addition to specific suggestions for different stakeholders—administrators, teachers, students, families, and community members—there is a detailed checklist to help the reader begin taking action.

There are also two appendixes to support readers as they seek to better understand and work against this issue. Appendix A comprises a list of available resources for use in classrooms with students and professional development workshops. This appendix provides information about cost, length of time, and a summary of the key points of information included for each book, film, or training manual. Appendix B is a glossary of terms to help the reader grasp new words and concepts introduced in this book.

CONCLUSION

This book has grown out of 15 years of professional and personal experiences working and conducting research in schools. I left the classroom because as a teacher I felt frustrated by the lack of leadership provided by my administrators and lack of concern demonstrated by my colleagues for addressing an issue that has such a significant impact on students' feelings of success and safety in school. I hope that the research and recommendations gathered in this book will help other educators, families, and community members who are working to make their schools safer and more inclusive for all students. It is challenging to try to change deeply entrenched attitudes and behaviors in a school community. However, this is the work that needs to be done to end the forms of bullying and harassment discussed in this book. Don't lose hope. It can be done. Together, we can make a difference in the lives of students. Good luck and *Bon Courage*!

Dedication

Dedicated to the memory of Joe Kincheloe:
Inspirational scholar, respected mentor, passionate musician,
and beloved friend.
Thank you for your words, your joy, and your love.
We miss you.

Acknowledgments

I must begin by thanking the many students and colleagues who have impacted me during my years of classroom teaching. Emily Novak brought the problem of gendered harassment to my attention during my first year of teaching in 1994, and my colleague and friend, John Spear, encouraged me to learn more about how to address these issues in schools and went on to do amazing work in this area with GLSEN (Gay, Lesbian and Straight Education Network). Many other students showed me their strength and resilience as they lived through forms of gendered harassment at our schools. I am sorry I wasn't able to do more at the time. I would specifically like to acknowledge Liz Morrow, Sue Hargrove, Jacob Heal, Mo Keita, and Jodi Gosse as well as the girls in Lindsay Dorm and on the hockey team. You gave me many important insights into our school's culture and how you experienced it. I loved working with you all.

This book would not have been possible without the eight teachers who volunteered their precious time to contribute to this study. They spoke openly, reflected deeply, and gave fully of themselves to this project. I truly enjoyed listening to their stories and am grateful for all I have learned through them.

This book emerged from my graduate studies at McGill University. This work was guided and influenced by many people there, so I apologize if I have not named everyone specifically. There are many professors and graduate students who offered informal advice and support that helped me navigate the complicated waters of doctoral study. The two paid student research assistants who helped with transcribing the interviews, Liz Airton and Natalie Kouri-Towe, helped move the data analysis process along smoothly. My graduate student colleagues were also an incredible source of support. I need to mention a few in particular: Gia Deleveaux, Tim Dougherty, Carmen LaVoie, and Andrea Sterzuk. Thanks for editing drafts of my writings and offering feedback and guidance along the way. I would also like to thank the supportive professors I worked with: Lynn Butler-Kisber, Steve Jordan, Joe Kincheloe, Bronwen Low, Claudia Mitchell, Anthony

Paré, and Shaheen Shariff. I am also grateful to Shari Brotman in the School of Social Work for her mentorship and guidance and the valuable research experience I gained while working with her. Finally, I must extend my most sincere gratitude to my supervisor, Shirley Steinberg, for her friendship as well as her emotional and professional support.

I am also grateful to the staff at Teachers College Press for their assistance in making this book possible. Most important, I must thank my editor, Marie Ellen Larcada, for working with me on this proposal and manuscript so it could reach a wider audience. I learned much from her during this process and appreciate that she saw potential in this manuscript and was willing to work with a scholar so early in her career.

Finally, I must thank my family for their enduring love and support during this process. My parents provided me with the encouragement and support I needed to return to graduate school. Their understanding and high expectations have enabled me to grow and challenge myself and others in important ways. Thank you for making this journey possible. Also, my deepest love and gratitude go to my wife, Veronika Lesiuk, who has been incredibly patient, loving, and supportive. In addition to endless hours of editing she gave freely of her time, her heart, and her mind to help everything I do become better than it would have been without her input.

CHAPTER 1

The Effects of Gender on Bullying and Harassment

Bullying and harassment in schools are persistent, prevalent, and commonly misunderstood. Many schools have been trying to combat violence and harassing behaviors by implementing blanket bullying policies that do little to specifically address the underlying school climate and culture that allow these behaviors to persist (Soutter & McKenzie, 2000; Walton, 2004). The long-term impacts on individuals targeted for harassment are well documented and severe: Lower academic performance, absenteeism, drug and alcohol abuse, and suicidal behaviors have all been linked to victims of schoolyard bullies (Bond, Carlin, Thomas, Rubin, & Patton, 2001; Rigby & Slee, 1999; Sharp, 1995). Students who are targets of sexual and homophobic harassment as well as harassment for gender nonconformity have been identified as being at even greater risk for these harmful behaviors and leaving school (California Safe Schools Coalition, 2004; Kosciw & Diaz, 2006; Reis & Saewyc, 1999; Williams, Connolly, Pepler, & Craig, 2005).

This book presents information about the problem of gender, bullying, and harassment in schools and provides resources and interventions to help educators better understand the possible roots of these behaviors. By placing the gendered dimensions of behaviors commonly viewed as bullying as central, I aim to make explicit how gender, specifically the public performance of masculinities and femininities, shapes harmful behavior in schools and how educators and concerned adults can work to reduce the negative impacts of these all-too-common schoolyard behaviors.

THE DIFFERENCES BETWEEN BULLYING,
HARASSMENT, AND GENDERED HARASSMENT

Gendered harassment is a term used to describe any behavior that acts to shape and police the boundaries of traditional gender norms: heterosexual

1

masculinity and femininity. It is related to, but different from, bullying. *Bullying* is defined as behavior that repeatedly and over time intentionally inflicts injury on another individual (Olweus, 1993), whereas *harassment* includes biased behaviors that have a negative impact on the target or the environment (Land, 2003). Although forms of bullying and harassment may overlap, they are different in two important ways. First, bullies intentionally inflict injury, whereas people guilty of harassment may be intentionally or unintentionally creating a hostile climate through their words and actions. Second, since harassment can target a specific individual or a group such as girls, students with disabilities, or gays and lesbians, the impact of harassing behaviors can be much more widespread. Bullying is targeted at a single individual. Harassment poisons an entire school community. Forms of gendered harassment include (hetero)sexual harassment, sexual orientation harassment, and harassment for gender nonconformity (or transphobic harassment). These three forms of harassment are interconnected because the harassers' behaviors reinforce expected cultural norms for boys and girls and punish students who don't fit the ideals of traditional (heterosexual) gender roles (Larkin, 1994; Martino, 1995; Martino & Pallotta-Chiarolli, 2003; Renold, 2002; G. W. Smith & Smith, 1998; Stein, 1995). Figure 1.1 presents how bullying, harassment, and gendered harassment are related.

Although physical bullying is often the most obvious form of aggression that is acknowledged and addressed in schools, verbal bullying and harassment are also prevalent and often ignored, even though they have been found to be quite damaging to students as well. Hoover and Juul (1993) found in their study on bullying that repeated verbal attacks by peers are as devastating as infrequent cases of physical abuse. Most bullying policies and interventions are not designed to get at the more persistent and insidious forms of harassment that occur in schools. Bullying and zero-tolerance policies tend to ignore the cultural and societal factors that lead to violence in schools. These policies and related intervention programs also ignore incidents of psychological violence (Walton, 2004). While I do not wish to ignore the painful experiences that victims of physical harassment and violence endure, this book will primarily address the emotional violence caused by the more insidious and often ignored issue of gendered harassment that is verbal and psychological in nature.

UNDERSTANDING THE SCOPE OF THE PROBLEM

I began investigating this problem as a result of my experiences as a high school teacher in the United States observing the hostile climate that existed for *gay, lesbian, bisexual, and transgender* (GLBT) students in my school.

Figure 1.1. The Relation of Bullying, Harassment, and Gendered Harassment

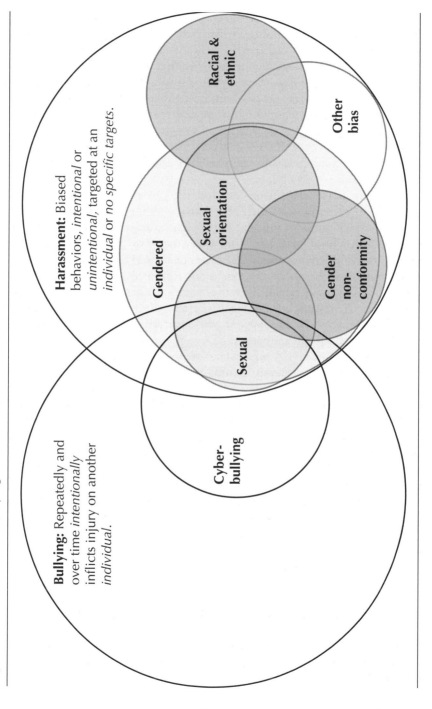

Harassment: Biased behaviors, *intentional or unintentional,* targeted at an *individual or no specific targets.*

Racial & ethnic

Other bias

Sexual orientation

Gendered

Gender non-conformity

Sexual

Cyber-bullying

Bullying: Repeatedly and over time *intentionally* inflicts injury on another *individual.*

During my first year of teaching, I observed a very bright and athletic student—a leader in the school—descend into depression, drug use, and skipping classes as a result of how her peers were treating her. She had fallen in love with a young woman she had met that summer, and her classmates were quick to show their disapproval. In addition to being excluded from her peer group, she was verbally harassed on a regular basis. This change in her school experience was enough to send a previously strong and confident young woman into a downward spiral of self-doubt and dangerous behavior. As a young teacher who wanted to support this student, I felt frustrated and angry by what the other teachers allowed to happen in their presence at the school.

As I investigated this problem further, I learned that although GLBT youth are commonly targeted for harassment, they are not the only ones suffering from the homophobic and (hetero)sexist climate of the school. Any student whose behavior is perceived to be different in some way can be isolated and harassed using anti-gay insults (O'Conor, 1995; Renold, 2002; Rofes, 1995; G. W. Smith & Smith, 1998), and any student who wishes to assert and defend his/her place in the *heteronormative* social order of the school must engage in (hetero)sexualized *discourse* that includes various forms of gendered harassment (Duncan, 1999; Martino & Berrill, 2003; Renold, 2003).

Students who are harassed in their schools have been found to be more likely to skip school, abuse drugs and alcohol, and have a higher rate of suicidal ideation (Bagley, Bolitho, & Bertrand, 1997; Irving & Parker-Jenkins, 1995; Rigby & Slee, 1999; Sharp, 1995; Slee, 1995). Most of these students perceive school as a dangerous place, and this perception causes significant damage to their level of engagement in the school community. One group of students that is regularly targeted in schools is GLBT youth (California Safe Schools Coalition, 2004; Kosciw & Diaz, 2006; Reis, 1999; Reis & Saewyc, 1999).

In a national phone survey with youth in the United States, the National Mental Health Association (2002) found that 50% of the respondents reported that students in their school who were gay would be bullied most or all of the time. In another U.S. survey, 91% of GLBT students report hearing homophobic remarks in school frequently or often (GLSEN, 2001). What is disturbing about this trend is not only its prevalence but also the lack of educators' effective intervention to stop this problem. In the Gay, Lesbian, and Straight Education Network (GLSEN) 2001 School Climate Survey, 83% of GLBT youth said that their teachers rarely or never intervened when hearing homophobic remarks (GLSEN, 2001). In a more recent study in California, students were asked how often they heard biased remarks (sex, sexual orientation, gender expression, religion, race, disability) and how often teachers intervened. The two forms of verbal harassment that students reported hearing the most were based on *sexual orientation* and *gender presentation*. These were also the two forms that students reported teachers were least likely to interrupt (California Safe Schools Coalition, 2004).

These studies indicate that educators are not adequately intervening in these forms of harassment. This inaction on the part of educators teaches students that the institution of the school—and by extension society as a whole—condones such activity. By teaching students that all forms of gendered harassment are tolerated, the school effectively supports the discriminatory attitudes that cause it to happen in the first place. As democratic institutions in a diverse and changing society, schools must teach about the causes of such harmful attitudes and work to reduce the impacts of them on their students. In so doing, we will be able to more effectively work to reduce prejudice and violence in schools. I will now address each of these forms of harassment in-depth to understand them more fully: sexual orientation harassment, harassment for gender nonconformity (or transphobic harassment), and (hetero)sexual harassment.

SEXUAL ORIENTATION HARASSMENT

Sexual orientation harassment, also known as homophobic harassment, is any behavior, hidden or obvious, that reinforces negative attitudes toward gay, lesbian, and bisexual people. The most common form of this harassment is verbal in nature and includes the use of anti-gay language as insults (e.g., "that's so gay," "don't be such a fag"), anti-gay jokes, and behaviors that ridicule gays and lesbians (such as affecting the speech and walk of a stereotypically effeminate gay man to get a laugh). The prevalence of this discourse in schools allows homophobic attitudes to develop and grow as students learn that this language is tacitly condoned by educators who fail to intervene when it is used. As George Smith explains:

> The local practices of the ideology of "fag" are never penalized or publicly condemned. Explicitly homophobic ridicule in sports contexts goes unremarked. Effective toleration of the ideology of "fag" among students and teachers condemns gay students to the isolation of "passing" or ostracism and sometimes to a life of hell in school. (G. W. Smith & Smith, 1998, p. 332)

This condemnation of gay students in schools is pervasive and damaging. The isolation and vulnerability experienced by these students is exacerbated by the refusal of teachers and administrators to intervene on their behalf. Many students' experiences support Smith's assertion. In the Human Rights

Watch (Bochenek & Brown, 2001) study *Hatred in the Hallways*, several students spoke of similar experiences:

> Nothing was done by the administration. A guy screamed "queer" down the hall in front of the principal's office, but nothing happened to him. The teachers—yeah, the teachers could have seen what was going on. Nothing happened. (p. 39)

> In addition to abuse from her peers, one of her teachers also harassed her verbally, calling her a lesbian and linking her sexual orientation to her performance in class. "He'd say, 'Well, if you weren't a lesbian you might pass this class,' or 'If you'd get your head out from between those girls' thighs, maybe you'd pass.' The message was I would be so much better off if I weren't gay." (pp. 65–66)

These stories are not exceptional. In the GLSEN's National School Climate Survey (2001), 84% of GLBT youth reported being verbally harassed in school and 64.3% reported feeling unsafe. These students were also targets for school graffiti, vandalism, and ostracism that often left them at high risk for depression, dropping out of school, and suicide (California Safe Schools Coalition, 2004; GLSEN, 2001; Reis & Saewyc, 1999). On a more positive note, these students reported less harassment and increased feelings of school safety when a teacher intervened sometimes or often to stop name-calling (California Safe Schools Coalition, 2004).

In addition to the risks that GLBT youth face in schools as a result of this homophobic climate, students who are perceived to be gender nonconforming are also frequently targeted in schools. Harassment for behavior that transcends narrow gender norms is one that is often lumped together with homophobic harassment, but it is important to investigate separately so as not to further confuse existing misconceptions of *gender identity* and expression with sexual orientation.

HARASSMENT FOR GENDER NONCONFORMITY OR TRANSPHOBIC HARASSMENT

Harassment for *gender nonconformity* is underresearched but important to understand. It happens when students are harassed because of their *gender expression*, or their public performance of masculinity or femininity. According to the California Safe Schools study, 27% of students surveyed reported being harassed for gender nonconformity (California Safe Schools Coalition, 2004). Due to prevalent stereotypes of gay men and lesbian women who transgress traditional gender norms, people whose behavior challenges popular notions of masculinity and femininity are often perceived to be gay themselves. This is a dangerous assumption to make, as it mistakenly confuses the concepts of sexual orientation and gender identity. Many adults also engage in this flawed logic due to their misunderstandings of gender and sexual orientation. There is insufficient room in this volume to fully explore the notions of *sex, gender*, and *sexual orientation*, but suffice it to say that each of these identities is distinct and may be expressed in a variety of ways. For example, although many biological females (sex) identify as heterosexual (sexual orientation) women (gender identity), that does not mean that it is the only possible combination of orientations and identities. By allowing students to believe that there is only one set of identities that are acceptable, schools reinforce traditional notions of heterosexual masculinity and femininity that create hostile school environments and effectively reduce educational opportunities for all students.

Research has demonstrated that more rigid adherence to traditional sex roles correlates with more negative attitudes and violent behaviors toward gays and lesbians (Bufkin, 1999; Whitley, 2001). When boys disengage from the arts and girls avoid appearing too athletic or assertive, it is often the result of gender stereotypes exerting their powerful influence over the students in the form of teasing and jokes. The threat of being perceived as a "sissy" or a "tomboy" and the resulting homophobic backlash limits the ways in which students participate in school life. Martino & Pallotta-Chiarolli (2003) describe an interview with a student who was harassed for his interest in art: "On his way to school one morning a group of boys at the back of the bus from one of the local high schools started calling him names. Initially, he was targeted as an 'art boy' because he was carrying an art file. But the harassment escalated and they began calling him 'fag boy' "(p. 52).

Unfortunately, our society's tendency to devalue qualities associated with femininity make this gender performance harder on nonconforming boys than on nonconforming girls. Schools tend to place a higher value on strength, competitiveness, aggressiveness, and being tough: qualities generally viewed to be masculine. Being creative, caring, good at school, and quiet, however, are often considered to be feminine qualities and are viewed by many as signs of weakness—particularly in boys. In their study on masculinities in Australian schools, researchers found that although many boys were able to perform the techniques of literacy, such as reading and writing, acting out an "appropriate" masculinity often prevented them from showing these abilities. Boys didn't want to appear good at school because it would be perceived as a threat to their masculinity, which they asserted through athleticism, physical strength, and heterosexual talk and behaviors (Martino & Pallotta-Chiarolli, 2003). They also discuss how this plays out in physical education: Activities in which both men and women can excel, such as dance and gymnastics, are not as esteemed as those sports that encourage boys to act out in more traditionally masculine ways, such as rugby and football. It is not surprising, then, that bullying studies report that typical victims are described as physically weak, timid, anxious, sensitive, and shy. In contrast, bullies are described as being physically strong, aggressive, dominating, and impulsive (Hoover & Juul, 1993).

It is difficult to effectively intervene to stop overt bullying when the qualities that these bullies embody are the ones that are most valued by many and demonstrate a form of power that is generally esteemed in a *patriarchal* society. *Hegemonic* masculinity (Connell, 1995), the embodiment of the dominant, tough, competitive, athletic male, is the standard of behavior in schools and any variation tends to be punished by the peer group (Robinson, 2005; Stoudt, 2006). Covert bullying, which is more common among groups of girls, uses the form of power most available to and acceptable for women: social relationships (Brown, 2003; Simmons, 2002). Though many researchers understand bullying as antisocial behavior, the fact that bullies usually hold social power and get what they want out of such activity shows that they have learned to assert their strength in ways that benefit them. As Canadian scholar Gerald Walton (2004) argues, understanding bullying as antisocial behavior "is a misconceptualization because it affords dominance and social status and is often rewarded and supported by other children. It may not be nice, but it is, nevertheless, very social" (p. 33).

The *social constructs* of ideal masculinity and femininity are at the core of much bullying behavior. As a result of this, students report that schools are safer for gender nonconforming girls (California Safe Schools Coalition, 2004). The pressure on boys to conform to traditional notions of masculinity is great, and the risk of being perceived as gay is an effective threat in policing the boundaries of acceptable behavior. One male student described its impacts on his life:

> When I was in elementary school, I did a lot of ballet. I was at the National Ballet School one summer. And that sort of stigma (laugh) which I never thought was a stigma, or could be a stigma, but which became a stigma, followed me into high school. And that was followed with comments continually—"fag," you know, "fag." I think that was actually one of the reasons why I eventually gave up ballet was just because of the constant harassment, and also pursuing other interests. But I think that was at the back of my mind a lot of the time with the harassment, and realizing that they're right. That's what I was. I knew that that's what I was. (quoted in G. W. Smith & Smith, 1998, p. 322)

This student describes how he eventually gave up his training as a ballet dancer as a result of the stigma that was attached to it by his peers. When students are limited from developing their strengths because of the climate of the school, then the educational system has failed that student and many others.

In order to assert their heterosexual masculinity, many boys engage in overt forms of heterosexualized behaviors, as this is seen as the best way to avoid being called gay. One gay student gave the following example:

> You know when all the guys would be making girl jokes, you'd have to go along with them, as much as you tried not to, you still had to chuckle here and there to not raise suspicion . . . very frequently, jokingly, some students would say to other students—when they didn't necessarily conform to all the jokes and the way of thinking of women students—they'd say, "what, you're not gay, are you?" (quoted in G. W. Smith & Smith, 1998, p. 324)

In this excerpt, the student explains how he feels obliged to participate in the (hetero)sexual harassment of his female peers in order to protect himself from being the target of homophobic harassment. The pressure to participate in these oppressive practices works in multiple ways to assert the power of hegemonic masculinity: it engages additional participants in the sexual harassment of females and labels those who choose not to participate as gay. This pressure to conform to ideals of hegemonic masculinity is at the core of most gendered harassment. This example provides a helpful segue to discuss the third area of gendered harassment: (hetero)sexual harassment.

(HETERO)SEXUAL HARASSMENT

Sexual harassment in schools has been the subject of research and public conversation since the early 1990s (Corbett, Gentry, & Pearson, 1993; Larkin, 1994; Louis Harris & Associates, 1993; Stein, Linn, & Young, 1992). In spite of this, it is still prevalent in schools. *Verbal harassment* is the most common form of sexual harassment reported by students, and female students experience more frequent and more severe forms of sexual harassment than males (Lee, Croninger, Linn, & Chen, 1996). Terms such as *bitch*, *baby*, *chick*, and *fucking broad* are commonly used in schools by male students as ways to assert masculinity by degrading female peers (Larkin, 1994). Another common way for males to perform their masculinity is to engage in heterosexual discourse by sexually objectifying their female peers and discussing sexual acts they would like to engage in or have already engaged in (Duncan, 1999; Eder, 1997; Larkin, 1994; Stein, 2002). This is often done near the female students but is not always directed at them, thus creating a space where women are targeted and objectified with no outlet for response or complaint of tangible harm. This activity creates a hostile climate for most students (Stein, 1995; Wood, 1987). It is generally not stopped by teachers, and sometimes it is encouraged by their tacit participation. Students reported that male teachers might "laugh along with the guys" (Larkin, 1994, p. 270) or support the comments and even blame the victim, as demonstrated in the following incident:

I took a photography class, and the majority of the class was boys. . . . One day I was in the room alone and one of the boys came in. When I went to leave he grabbed me and threw me down and grabbed my breast. I felt I was helpless but I punched him and he ran out. The teacher (who was a man) came in and yelled at me. When I tried to explain why I had hit him the teacher told me I deserved it because I wore short skirts. I was sent to the principal and I had to serve detention. I didn't want to tell the principal because I feared he would do the same and tell me it was my fault. I felt so alone. Everyday I had to go to class and face it. No girl should have to be uncomfortable because of what she wears or how she acts. (quoted Stein, 1995, p. 148)

This example shows how teachers can exacerbate situations by reinforcing the behavior of the offending students. In this case, not only did the teacher not intervene in the sexual harassment, but he added to it by commenting on her attire and stating that she "deserved it." With teachers role-modeling and reinforcing such behaviors, it is clear that a new approach to preventing sexual harassment in schools is needed.

Although sexual harassment, by definition, is sexual in nature, I have included it as a form of gendered harassment due the theoretical understanding of its roots: the public performance of traditional heterosexual gender roles. In its most commonly understood form, sexual harassment is directed by a male toward a female and ranges from comments, gestures, leers, or "invitations" of a sexual nature to physical touching, grabbing, rubbing, and violent assault such as rape. I will continue to focus here on the more subtle and insidious behaviors where the harassers assert their gender role through acts of domination and humiliation, since physically violent and intrusive acts are ones that generally get a response from school authorities regardless of motive or context.

Although females are most commonly targeted, it is important to acknowledge that men can also be victims of sexual harassment, much of it from other men, and it tends to be homophobic in nature. Young women may also be implicated in such behaviors, and it is most commonly exhibited as verbal insults directed toward other females as a result of competition for boyfriends or friendship groups (Duncan, 2004).

Sexual harassment has been described as a way of understanding how patriarchy works: a way men continue to assert their power over women. Though this is a useful place to begin, it is important to stretch our understanding of this problem to include how valorized forms of traditionally masculine behaviors are allowed to be practiced and performed over the devalued forms of traditional notions of femininity. These gender roles are constructed within a *heterosexual matrix* (Butler, 1990) that only allows for a single dominant form of *compulsory heterosexuality* (Rich, 1978/1993). As long as these attitudes and behaviors continue to go unchallenged, then schools will continue to be sites where youths are harassed out of an education. In order to prevent this from continuing, we must learn effective strategies for intervention that will help educators create schools where such discriminatory attitudes and behaviors will be replaced by more inclusive notions of respect, equality, and understanding.

CONCLUSION

My experiences as a classroom teacher are what led me to pursue a deeper understanding of the phenomenon of gendered harassment in schools. The frustration I felt at the inaction of my colleagues and the pervasive nature of the sexual harassment, sexual orientation harassment, and harassment for gender nonconformity led me to study the factors that influence how teachers understand and respond to gendered harassment in schools. The information presented in this book aims to provide educators the information and resources necessary to transform their own school cultures.

Students who are targets for gendered harassment tend to suffer silently and internalize the harmful messages embedded in the persistent insults and jokes that permeate many school cultures. The focus on bullying and physical aggression has brought into perspective some important concerns but has also obscured many others. By using vague terms such as *bullying* and *name-calling*, scholars and educators avoid examining the underlying power dynamics that such behaviors build upon and reinforce. When policies and interventions don't name and explore systems of power and privilege, they effectively reinforce the status quo. Educators must understand that when insults and jokes are used to marginalize groups who have experienced systemic discrimination, the damage goes beyond the harm to individual students. These discourses normalize and give authority to the invisible structures of social power and leave many students feeling hurt, excluded, and limited in their chances for educational success.

It is essential for students, teachers, school counselors, administrators, and parents to learn to see and critically examine the impacts of gendered harassment in schools and develop tools to work against it. By examining bullying and harassment together and explicitly addressing the underlying *homophobia, transphobia,* and *(hetero)sexism,* we will be able to create more systemic approaches to addressing violence in schools. The following chapters will provide educators a foundation for understanding how to change the culture of their schools by learning how to see, understand, and transform practices, policies, procedures, and curricula that may teach and reinforce biases based on sex, gender, and sexual orientation.

CHAPTER 2

What We Know About Gender, Bullying, and Harassment

Scholarship investigating aggression between peers in school has been growing steadily since Norwegian researcher Dan Olweus published the first study on bullying, *Aggression in the Schools: Bullies and Whipping Boys*, in 1978. Several studies emerged in the 1980s and early 1990s that used Olweus's questionnaire in other countries and established his definitions and research methods as the most influential in this field. The result of this dominant influence has been to establish a body of knowledge about bullying that is widely recognized in many countries around the world, but one that has created important blind spots in how educators understand and respond to bullying in their own schools. This chapter presents the main trends in and findings from bullying and harassment studies in secondary schools. Further, it offers an analysis of how this knowledge has impacted popular understandings of and interventions for reducing bullying and harassment.

In order to provide the reader with a basic understanding of what we currently know about gender, bullying, and harassment, it is important to investigate four related but distinct areas of research: bullying, sexual harassment, sexual orientation harassment, and cyber-bullying in secondary schools. They are presented in this order to assist the reader in understanding the chronology of the research and how earlier studies have influenced later work.

BULLYING

Dan Olweus published his first study on the problem of bullying in Norway in 1978 and has consistently set the agenda for research in this field by defining bullying, structuring how researchers study the problem, and creating interventions and evaluations of programs to reduce bullying in schools. The impact that his work has had in influencing the direction of this field of study is evidenced in how regularly his studies are cited in other research. In an analysis of 34 bullying articles published since 1990, his work was referenced in 26 of them. The 26 studies that cite Olweus's work use his definition of bullying and apply his approach to identifying how often students experienced bullying and its impact on their well-being. These studies were conducted in countries around the world, including New Zealand (Adair, Dixon, Moore, & Sutherland, 2000; Coggan, Bennett, Hooper, & Dickinson, 2003), Australia (Bond et al., 2001; Rigby & Cox, 1996; Rigby, Cox, & Black, 1997; Rigby & Slee, 1999; Slee, 1995), Malta (Borg, 1999), the United Kingdom (Boulton, Bucci, & Hawker, 1999; Boulton, Trueman, & Flemington, 2002; Mynard & Stephen, 2000; Naylor & Cowie, 1999; Naylor, Cowie, & del Rey, 2001; Schafer et al., 2004; Sharp, 1995), the United States (Batsche & Knoff, 1994; Gruber & Fineran, 2008; Hazler, Hoover, & Oliver, 1991; Hoover & Juul, 1993; Land, 2003; Nolin, Davies, & Chandler, 1996; Pelligrini & Long, 2002), and Norway (Olweus, 1996). These studies consistently used the following definition of bullying created by Olweus:

> A student is being bullied or victimized when he or she is exposed, repeatedly and over time, to negative actions on the part of one or more other students . . . it is a negative action when someone intentionally inflicts, or attempts to inflict, injury or discomfort on another. . . . Negative actions can be carried out by words (verbally), for instance, by threatening, taunting, teasing, and calling names. It is a negative action when somebody hits, pushes, kicks, pinches or restrains another—by physical contact. It is also possible to carry out negative actions without the use of words or physical contact, such as by making faces or dirty gestures, intentionally excluding someone from a group, or refusing to comply with another person's wishes. (1993, p. 9)

These studies reported between 9% (Olweus, 1993), 33% (Bond et al., 2001), and 58% (Adair et al., 2000) of students as victims of bullying at school. The wide variation in reported rates of bullying may be attributed to how survey questions were phrased, what time period was being investigated (entire school career, the past year, the past month), and how the data were analyzed and reported.

Researchers also found a large number of negative impacts associated with being the victim of bullying. These studies reported that students who were victims of bullying also reported symptoms of anxiety, depression, stress, hopelessness, and low self-esteem and were more likely to attempt self-harming behaviors and suicide (Bond et al., 2001; Coggan et al., 2003).

Studies in the United States

Recent bullying research conducted in the United States has addressed several topics, including age-related changes in bullying (Pelligrini & Long, 2002); differences among teasing, bullying, and sexual harassment (Land, 2003); and frequencies of bullying as compared to sexual harassment (Gruber & Fineran, 2008). Pelligrini and Long (2002) studied students during the transition period from elementary to middle school and found that bullying and aggression initially increased and then decreased over time, with more boys than girls engaging in aggressive behavior (2002). Deborah Land (2003) found that students generally did not consider verbal comments and non-physical behaviors to be bullying or sexual harassment.

Most recently, Gruber and Fineran (2008) published the first study to examine the prevalence and impacts of bullying and sexual harassment behaviors in the same study. This is valuable information for educators and scholars because it provides a common frame of reference for understanding these overlapping issues. They found that more students experienced bullying (52%) than sexual harassment (34%) and that boys and girls experienced similar levels of both bullying (53% vs. 51%, respectively) and harassment (36% vs. 34%, respectively). Where they did find a difference was in students who identified as gay, lesbian, bisexual, or questioning their sexual orientation (GLBQ). They found that GLBQ students experienced more bullying (79% vs. 50%) and more sexual harassment (71% vs. 32%) than non-GLBQ-identified students.

This study also examined the impact of bullying and sexual harassment on the health of students. It found that girls and GLBQ students generally have poorer health (self-esteem, mental and physical health, and trauma symptoms) during middle and high school. Finally, they concluded that sexual harassment has a more severe impact than bullying on a student's overall health. Their findings led them to conclude that "the current trend of focusing on [bullying], or else subsuming harassment under bullying, draws attention away from a significant health risk" (Gruber & Fineran, 2008, p. 9) and that schools need to include sexual harassment interventions as a distinct focus.

Teachers' Perspectives

Internationally, several studies have been conducted that attempt to understand bullying from the teacher's perspective. Mark Borg (1998) conducted a study in Malta that developed an understanding of the bully–victim problem from the teacher's point of view. In this study, cruelty/bullying was ranked as the second most serious behavior behind drug abuse. Sex stereotypes had a strong influence in what behaviors teachers deemed as inappropriate. Female teachers were more concerned with "moral forms of behaviors" (such as masturbation, cruelty/bullying, obscene notes, and lying), whereas male teachers were more focused on "disruptive forms of behaviors (such as disorderliness, defiance/challenge, interrupting, restlessness)" (p. 76). This gender difference points to the influence of teachers' own identities and experiences on how they perceive and respond to student behaviors in school. In a similar study conducted in the United Kingdom, researchers reported that teachers were "generally sympathetic towards victims, although sympathy diminished with increasing length of service" (Boulton, 1997). Boulton also found that teachers were not confident in their abilities to deal with bullying and that a large percentage (87%) wanted more training.

Most recently, an Australian study (Ellis & Shute, 2007) reported that a teacher's own moral orientation (justice- or care-oriented) influenced how and when teachers intervened in bullying. They also determined that the perceived severity of the incident increased the likelihood of teacher intervention. An interesting gender variation was also reported from this study: male teachers were less likely to intervene in cases of verbal harassment and social exclusion despite research indicating that these forms can have more lasting harm on students (Bond et al., 2001; Salmon & West, 2000; Slee, 1995).

Intervention Programs

Several studies have been conducted to evaluate bullying intervention programs. These program evaluations described several different approaches to reducing bullying in school: an educational video intervention (Boulton & Flemington, 1996), an implementation of a new bullying policy (Cartwright, 1995), a school-based social work program (Bagley & Pritchard, 1998), and two peer support programs designed to assist with conflict resolution (Cowie, 1998; Price & Jones, 2001). Each author reported an increased awareness of and discussions about bullying in the school; however, only Bagley and Pritchard's (1998) school social work program was able to demonstrate that it was able to reduce the incidence of bullying in the schools.

Olweus, on the other hand, reported success with his intervention programs conducted in Norway from 1983 to 1985 (Olweus, 1993) but notes that replication studies that were not as controlled showed less effectiveness (Olweus, 2003). The success of the Olweus Bullying Prevention Program has also been reported more recently by Black and Jackson (2007). Their research was unique in that they used observations to calculate bullying incidents rather than relying solely on student or teacher reports. This study calculated bullying density in eight elementary and middle schools before program implementation and over 4 years of implementation. Their find-ings report that this program successfully reduced bullying density in some schools by up to 65% (from 65 incidents per 100 student hours to 36 inci-dents per 100 student hours).

Most recently, a team of researchers in the United States (Merrell, Gueld-ner, Ross, & Isava, 2008) conducted a meta-analysis of bullying interven-tion programs. In this study the team evaluated the findings of 16 different quantitative studies that measured the effectiveness of bullying intervention programs conducted between 1980 and 2004. The results of their analysis indicate that bullying prevention programs can have a positive effect on stu-dents' and teachers' perceptions, attitudes, and understandings of bullying behaviors but have little measurable effect on reducing the actual frequency and severity of bullying in a school. These findings indicate that there are some positive benefits to bullying intervention programs; however, the de-gree of implementation and longevity of the intervention are important fac-tors that influence long-term measurable effects on reducing bullying. Some of the more successful aspects of the above programs will be highlighted in the recommendations in Chapter 6.

Gender and Bullying

Most research that addresses gender and bullying has focused on the relative frequency and types of bullying experienced by girls and boys. Researchers have reported that boys bully more often than girls, either in groups or as individuals, and that boys are also victimized more frequently (Beaty & Alexeyev, 2008; Olweus, 1993; Siann, Callaghan, Glissove, Lockhart, & Rawson, 1994). However, much bullying research focuses on easily observ-able physical behaviors that tend to be more common among boys. Neil Duncan has contributed much to this area with his book *Sexual Bullying* (1999) and recent articles (2004, 2006). These projects investigated the sex-ualized element of much of the bullying that goes on in schools. His later works focused on bullying between girls, including accusations of being a lesbian or heterosexual promiscuity. Other research, such as Rachel Sim-mons's *Odd Girl Out* (2002) and Lyn Mikel Brown's *Girlfighting* (2003), also provide a more in-depth look at the types of covert and relational bully-ing that happens in girls' social groups, which is quite difficult for research-ers to observe and measure but clearly has lasting harmful impacts on the well-being of girls.

Gaps in Bullying Knowledge

The main weakness in the current trend of bullying studies is that they fail to explore and acknowledge the influences of larger social forces such as sexism, homophobia, and transphobia in understanding relationships of power and dominance in peer groups. They recognize various forms of verbal aggression but, with few exceptions, never explore the relationship they have with social biases and cultural norms. They address the issue of name-calling but never explore what names are being used to hurt and insult students. As the harassment studies will show, many of the insults used by bullies reinforce dominant notions of *euroheteropatriarchy* (Valdez, 2002) or White, masculine, heterosexual superiority. In the above articles, only a few made mention of gender and how aspects of masculinity and femininity might alter how bullying is performed and experienced by each gender (Cowie, 1998; Land, 2003; Naylor et al., 2001; Pelligrini & Long, 2002; Slee, 1995).

In order to move beyond the basic understandings bullying studies have constructed about these behaviors in schools, it is important to explore related research that has been designed to explore issues of harassment as well. By definition, harassment studies have a different perspective on aggression and social power in schools that addresses bias-related issues that will contribute to a better understanding of gender and harassment in schools.

SEXUAL HARASSMENT

Current harassment studies have primarily focused on the narrowly defined issue of heterosexual harassment of females by males. The earliest article that explored female students' experiences with sexual harassment was June Larkin's (1994) study, "Walking Through Walls: The Sexual Harassment of High School Girls." This study confirmed the pervasiveness of sexual harassment behaviors and how they had been normalized in schools due to the frequency of incidents, responses by male peers, and the silence around it in schools.

In 1996, Lee, Croninger, Linn, and Chen analyzed survey data initially reported by the American Association of University Women (AAUW)(Harris & Associates, 1993). Lee and colleagues concluded that harassment was disruptive for all students but had more severe impacts on girls and Black students due to the context of the school. They also concluded that harassed students experience academic and psychological problems, particularly those who are harassed most severely (Lee et al., 1996).

Only one article in this body of research made any specific mention of the potential links and impacts of homophobia and sexual harassment among students. Timmerman's (2003) study in the Netherlands offered a valuable framework for understanding this problem. She examined student– student harassment using a Culture Model that assumed that sexual harassment reflects the school culture due to the fact that it is a public phenomenon and occurs on a daily basis. She found that the Culture Model was relevant in describing both student–student harassment and teacher–student harassment. This means that the culture of the school accepts the public and persistent sexual harassment of female students by teachers and peers. Male students and teachers comprised an overwhelming majority of the perpetrators. Although male and female students were both targeted, girls were the objects of more persistent and severe harassment. Timmerman did add that sexual harassment of boys "tends to be more verbal and homophobic in nature" (p. 242).

The AAUW conducted a follow-up study in 2001, which also showed that harassment was occurring in public, in the presence of adults. The three most common sites where harassment was reported were hallways (64%), classroom (56%), and the gym or playing field or pool area (43%). This provides information that is different from that reported in many bullying studies, which indicate that bullying happens where there is minimal adult supervision. This fact indicates that forms of sexual harassment may be more public and widely accepted in schools (Harris Interactive, 2001). The AAUW studies were the first ones to also systematically investigate sexual orientation harassment. The findings from this aspect of their research are reported in the following section.

SEXUAL ORIENTATION HARASSMENT

The earliest published report that began documenting incidents of sexual orientation harassment in schools and its impacts on the targeted students was the study entitled *Hostile Hallways* conducted by Harris and Associates (1993) for the AAUW. This study included a question that asked if participants had ever been called gay or lesbian in school. This was the first quantitative data available on the prevalence of this problem. A follow-up study 8 years later (Harris Interactive, 2001) found that the one form of harassment that had increased since the previous study was calling another student gay or lesbian. Boys reported that this occurred twice as often (9% vs. 19%) and girls that it occurred three times as often (5% vs. 13%) as a decade earlier (p. 21), whereas most other forms of harassment had remained constant or decreased.

In 1995, the first study that made central the issue of sexual orientation harassment and other forms of homophobia in schools was published by the Safe Schools Coalition of Washington, U.S.A. (Reis, 1995). The researchers documented 50 different incidences of anti-gay harassment ranging from name-calling to beatings and rape. This study also confirmed several of the findings from the AAUW study, including the facts that harassment is usually a public event, most harassers are fellow students, most harassers are male, and in most cases adults do not take appropriate actions against the offender(s).

In 1999, a meta-analysis of eight large-scale studies representing the experiences of 83,000 youth (Reis & Saewyc, 1999) highlighted the fact that gay, lesbian, and bisexual (GLB) students were at higher risk for several dangerous behaviors as compared with their heterosexual peers. GLB youth were over four times more likely to have attempted suicide, three times more likely to have been injured or threatened with a weapon at school, and three times more likely to have missed school because of feeling unsafe (Reis & Saewyc).

That same year, the first study by the Gay, Lesbian, and Straight Education Network (GLSEN) on school climate for GLBT youth in U.S. schools was released. This report also highlighted the problem of adults failing to intervene effectively (GLSEN, 1999). Every 2 years GLSEN has conducted follow-up studies (GLSEN, 2001; Kosciw, 2004; Kosciw & Diaz, 2006). The most recent report shows that 64% of GLBT students reported being verbally harassed at school and 83% also reported that faculty or staff rarely or never intervened when present and homophobic remarks were made (Kosciw & Diaz, 2006, p. 4).

A study conducted by the California Safe Schools Coalition was the first published research to identify and include all aspects of gendered harassment: sexual, sexual orientation, and gender nonconformity. This study reported the frequency and impacts of harassment for gender nonconformity by identifying students who are targeted for being "not as masculine as other boys" or "not as feminine as other girls." This study found that harassment for gender nonconformity was "clearly related to actual or perceived sexual orientation" (p. 15) since 49% of students who were harassed for their sexual orientation were also harassed for gender nonconformity, whereas 27% of the overall student population reported experiencing harassment for "not being masculine enough" or "not being feminine enough."

In regard to teacher response, students reported that teachers or staff were "unlikely to intervene" to stop bias-motivated comments, particularly those related to sexual orientation and gender presentation (California Safe Schools Coalition, 2004). The most encouraging finding from this study is the fact that where students see teachers stop negative comments and slurs based on sexual orientation, they report less name-calling and stronger feelings of school safety. These are important findings, as they demonstrate the impact that effective intervention can have on the experiences of students in schools.

In 2003, a Massachusetts study identified key factors that improve the "sexual diversity climate" in schools for all students. The three elements of the program evaluated were (1) having a clear school policy that included sexual orientation in its nondiscrimination statement, (2) conducting staff training on issues related to homophobia and sexual orientation, and (3) having a student Gay-Straight Alliance. This last recommendation "is the aspect most strongly associated with positive sexual diversity climates" (Szlacha, 2003, p. 73). Unfortunately, the reported implementation levels of the Safe Schools Program in Massachusetts were quite low. Although this program was initiated in 1993, by 1998 only 21% of the schools had implemented all three recommendations. This indicates that even when there is strong policy support and institutional resource allocations for anti-homophobia programs, there may be other obstacles preventing their successful implementation.

Several qualitative studies have also been published describing the problem of sexual orientation harassment in schools and the impacts on targeted students. The common thread in these studies was the recognition that homophobia is prevalent in schools and that it has a variety of negative impacts on all students. The first of these studies was George Smith's article "The Ideology of 'Fag': The School Experience of Gay Students" (G. W. Smith & Smith, 1998). Smith explored how speech (graffiti, verbal abuse, anti-gay activities, etc.) informs the experience of gay teenagers in school. He concluded that "the social relations of heterosexuality and patriarchy dominate public space. Being gay is never spoken of positively (in these informants' experiences)" (p. 309). He describes how the institution of the school "often gives tacit approval" (p. 321) for anti-gay activities as well as how gender relations are experienced within the heterosexist context of the school.

Phoenix, Frosh, and Pattman's (2003) article "Producing Contradictory Masculine Subject Positions: Narratives of Threat, Homophobia and Bullying in 11–14 Year Old Boys" provides an understanding of masculinity and how it relates to bullying and homophobia. The authors concluded, "Boys in this study reported that teachers in the schools in which we worked did not define homophobic name calling as bullying and so did not impose sanctions on those who engaged in it" (p. 193).

These studies, which have explicitly addressed the problems of sexual orientation harassment and related forms of homophobia and transphobia in schools, fill an important gap in the current bullying and harassment literature. These authors present compelling findings that underline the importance of addressing issues related to sexual orientation and gender identity when working to reduce bullying and harassment in schools. A new form of bullying that has not been addressed in these studies has recently emerged in youth cultures: cyber-bullying.

CYBER-BULLYING

In the above studies on bullying and harassment, GLSEN's 2006 report was the only one to explicitly address the topic of cyber-bullying. The researchers defined it as "using an electronic medium, such as emails or text messages, to threaten or harm others" (Kosciw & Diaz, 2006, p. 27). According to their research, 41% of LGBT students had experienced this type of harassment in the past year. This is four times higher than the national average of 9% reported in a recent large-scale study conducted by the University of New Hampshire (Wolak, Mitchell, & Finkelhor, 2006). This reflects the higher victimization of GLBT youth in school reported by other studies (California Safe Schools Coalition, 2004; GLSEN & Harris Interactive, 2005; Gruber & Fineran, 2008; Williams et al., 2003).

Other research has shown strong links between bullying at school and cyber-bullying. Hinduja and Patchin (2008) found in an online survey that students who were bullies or victims at school were more likely to be involved in cyber-bullying as well. In a Canadian study, Li (2006) also found similarities to schoolyard bullying: males (22%) were more likely to be cyber-bullies than females (12%), and males and females reported being victimized online at similar rates (25% vs. 25.6%). Cyber-bullying is a very difficult phenomenon for educators to address, since much of it occurs outside of school, but it still has an impact on students' experiences at school (Agatston, Kowalski, & Limber, 2007; Dehue, Bolman, & Vollink, 2008; P. K. Smith, Mahdavi et al., 2008). It is somewhat different from schoolyard bullying in that it can be anonymous and can have broader impacts with the widespread dissemination of information through broadcast text messages, posted videos, and Web pages. However, these elements can make cyber-bullying easier to prove by documenting the exact nature of the interaction.

This area of bullying research is highly relevant to issues of gendered harassment, as researchers have noted that cyberspace is becoming an increasingly hostile environment, particularly for girls and GLBT youth who are targets for harassment online (Barak, 2005; Kosciw & Diaz, 2006; Shariff & Gouin, 2006). The emergence of new virtual spaces—such as discussion boards, blogs, instant messaging programs, and social networking sites such as Friendster, Facebook, and MySpace—have created new arenas in which youth interact and inevitably harass (Jenkins & Boyd, 2006). The increasing accessibility of these spaces from Internet-connected laptops, personal data assistants (PDAs), portable gaming devices, and cell phones just multiplies the potential contact points for bullying and harassment. This does not necessarily mean that this is outside the realm of educators' interventions. Boyd argues that the visibility and public forum of Internet interactions can actually "provide a window through which teen mentors can help combat [bullying, sexual teasing, and other peer-to-peer harassment]" (Jenkins & Boyd, 2006, p. 5). This form of online interaction is an important one for educators and researchers to be aware of as youth behaviors spill out of the schoolyard and into cyberspace.

CONCLUSION

There has been a significant amount of research related to the issue of bullying, but less so regarding gendered harassment in schools. The bulk of the bullying and harassment studies discussed here do not consider the work done by scholars in parallel fields, which has resulted in blind spots in our knowledge about bullying and harassment. The majority of bullying and harassment studies have focused on describing the problem from the students' perspective. This has been an important first step in order to better understand and call attention this problem in schools.

However, most of these studies miss an important aspect of life in schools, since they have not considered the impacts of gender, sex, and sexual orientation on the power dynamics present in bully–victim interactions. Although a few of these studies explore how boys and girls bully differently, these studies overwhelmingly ignore the larger sociocultural influences of sex, gender, and sexual orientation on students' lives and how students exercise power within their school communities and peer relationships. On the other hand, many of the harassment studies are framed with a feminist lens and have a central focus on power dynamics organized along gender lines, but they are usually constructed along the male–female heterosexual matrix and pay limited attention to sexual orientation harassment.

The research specifically addressing sexual orientation harassment has documented the problem over the past decade and provides a foundation for understanding the phenomenon of gendered harassment in schools. The studies presented in this chapter offer us an important starting point for the next wave in bullying and harassment research and education programs. It is essential to understand what is currently known about bullying and harassment in schools as well as what intervention and education programs show promise in order to move forward with new and integrated ways of addressing this problem.

CHAPTER 3

The Effects of School Culture on Bullying and Harassment

It was this very [European] macho kind of attitude. The kids
used a lot of homophobic language to insult one another.
—Male Teacher 1

It would be difficult to respond to [homophobic insults] because
they occur so much—they're part of the school culture.
—Female Teacher 2

Much research on bullying and harassment has acknowledged the powerful influence that the culture of the school has on either perpetuating or
reducing forms of bullying and harassment. This chapter introduces the
importance of reading and understanding school cultures when working to
end bullying and harassment. It will offer readers a model of how to ana-
lyze their own school's culture and how to identify key areas for education
and intervention.

Chapter 1 points out the importance of including gender in any examination of and response to bullying and harassment in schools. Unfortunately,
as Chapter 2 points out, most research in this field has focused on individual
student behaviors and ignored important social and cultural impacts such as
gender, sexual orientation, race, ethnicity, religion, and the school environment that also shape and inform student behaviors. These elements must be
considered when examining the formal and informal structures of a school.

EXTERNAL INFLUENCES: THE FORMAL AND
INFORMAL STRUCTURES OF THE SCHOOL

Schools are microcosms of the communities they serve and thus often reflect
the culture and values of the dominant group in the school. In order to better

understand a school community, it is important to systematically evaluate whether each element that comprises the formal and informal structures of the institution is promoting the stated values of the school. This section offers an approach to understanding how a school can reinforce values that support gendered harassment through its formal and informal structures. Examining a school's culture in this fashion can provide educators and community members a systematic and informative way to better understand and develop targeted approaches to improving it.

This section first outlines the external influences that shape how individuals view and respond to bullying and harassment in their schools. The *external* influences include *formal* (institutional) and *informal* (social) structures. They interact with individuals' *internal* influences to shape their experience of their school culture. Internal influences are the focus of Chapter 4. In interviews conducted with teachers and in the research literature, school culture emerged as a dominant theme that impacted teachers' experiences in schools and their perceived ability to successfully intervene in incidents of bullying, harassment, and, in particular, gendered harassment. School culture is created by many structures that fall into two main categories: formal and informal.

Formal Structures: Institutional Practices

Formal structures within the school have a significant impact in creating and sustaining school cultures. The formal structures that teachers said impacted their perceptions of their school culture were (1) official policies on student safety, nondiscrimination, diversity and equity, bullying, and harassment; (2) administrative procedures and administrators' official responses to incidents of bullying and harassment; (3) curriculum demands and teacher workloads; and (4) teacher education and training programs. Through the course of the interviews that I conducted for this book, it became clear that these formal structures interacted with the informal structures of the school culture to shape teachers' experiences and their stated abilities to address forms of gendered harassment.

Official Policies

Many schools and school districts do not have clear policies preventing forms of gendered harassment (Kosciw & Diaz, 2006; Meyer, 2008c; Rollini, 2003; P. K. Smith, Smith, Osborn, & Samara, 2008). In schools that do have such policies, they are often not clearly explained or effectively implemented. Unfortunately, without a systemwide effort to create, update, and implement policies, educators are left to rely on their individual knowledge and interpretations of how to address bullying and harassment. This is evidenced in how the teachers spoke of their schools' policies during interviews. One teacher did voice a belief that his school's policy on bullying was clear, yet an analysis of his school's documents did not identify any clear, published guidelines on how to address bullying. The rest of the teachers in the study did not share the belief that they had a clear understanding of their school's policies. For example, one teacher spoke of her experience with school policies in the following way:

> I'm not aware of any [policies]. If there [were any], it was never brought to our attention. There was never a policy that was given to us: This is what you need to do about bullying. There are *so* many policies that you're not going to know them unless someone makes a point of saying "this one's important." (Female Teacher 2)

A second teacher expressed similar frustration at the lack of guidance she received from school policies: "I just think it's really unfortunate that there are not specific policies or regulations that we follow when it comes to verbal harassment" (Female Teacher 3). This lack of familiarity with school policy was also reported by Sarkar & Lavoie (2006) in their examination of Quebec teachers' integration of the Ministry of Education's Intercultural Education Policy.

Teachers' lack of awareness and understanding of current school policies and related laws is significant in shaping how educators act. In a study on sexual harassment in the United States, Gloria Jones (2005) found that an understanding of Title IX legislation was an important factor that caused educators to take on an activist role in regard to cases of peer sexual harassment. Jones's findings indicate that a familiarity with existing formal laws and policies can act as a motivator for teachers to actively work to reduce incidents of peer harassment.

The teachers also used terms such as *supposed to be* or *apparently* when referring to school anti-bullying policies, which indicates that there was some awareness of existing bullying policies. However, this awareness did not translate into consistent action in schools, since these policies were not clearly communicated or systematically implemented in any school.

Administrative Procedures and Responses

When asked about administrative procedures and administrators' responses to bullying and harassment, teachers spoke about not feeling supported by their administrators and believing that often the discipline meted out for instances of student-on-student sexual or sexual orientation harassment was not sufficient. One teacher explained:

As far as discipline, how it's handled, I had to push for action when another kid called a kid "faggot." However, I know that in my school a racist comment was certainly not tolerated and it was dealt with immediately. (Male Teacher 5)

The teachers in this study generally did not trust their administrators to support their disciplinary actions and felt that they had to handle most non-violent discipline issues alone. They spoke consistently about their schools' strong and clear response to any kind of physical violence, but they felt that the administration did not want to be bothered with issues of verbal harassment or other forms of psychological torment. This is important in light of the findings of other studies that antisocial behavior (such as vandal-ism, aggression, and rule infractions) in students increases when administrative support is inconsistent and when there is an absence of follow-up from school leadership (Mayer, 1995). In their research, Mayer and colleagues found that clarity of expectations, support for teachers by the administration, and respect for individual student differences were three areas that contributed to building positive school climates.

Curricular and Workload Demands

Another theme brought up by all the teachers was the challenge they faced meeting the curricular and workload demands of their jobs. This was one of the most common obstacles that teachers felt prevented them from acting as consistently as they would like toward various forms of verbal harass-ment. Many teachers felt great pressure from their administration to cover the required amounts of curricular material, and the stresses placed on them by large classes and demanding courseloads caused them to ignore certain behaviors. One teacher explained:

[I don't stop name-calling] if I'm too tired, if there are set things I need to get through in a lesson. I know my lesson is going to take 60 minutes, I've only got 70 minutes to deliver it, I've got 10 minutes to waste. Right now my job is being a teacher and I have to get through the math before the end of the year. It's not on my priority list. (Male Teacher 1)

Another teacher echoed this feeling by saying, "Accountability and NCLB [No Child Left Behind] is always over our heads and it's a lot of pressure. It's tricky to make sure we're covering what we need to and what's going to be on the test" (Male Teacher 7).

Teachers are exhausted and overwhelmed by the professional demands placed on them and do not feel they are given the necessary support or resources to deal with everything they would like to address. They are frustrated by these limitations, but none critiqued the formal structures of the school that caused them to feel overwhelmed. They spoke as if it were simply the reality that must be dealt with. When asked to suggest changes that could improve their ability to address bullying and harassment, no teacher mentioned reducing class sizes, limiting the number of class preparations, or adding educational assistants to alleviate some of these demands on their time and energy. This may suggest that teachers have a very limited sense of control over their school environment. By dealing with behavior issues only within the microstructures of their classrooms rather than addressing the macrostructures of the school, they are extremely limited in what they can do to improve student safety and school climate.

Teacher Education and Training

Most teachers felt that their teacher education programs did not sufficiently prepare them to address incidents of gendered harassment or bullying. Further, they did not feel that they had many opportunities to pursue additional training in this area because they were encouraged to do professional development primarily in their area of instruction. One teacher spoke about how her teacher training impacted how she viewed behaviors in her school:

> [I never got any] training in school [on] bullying. I do not think that we ever studied anything related to that. . . . I don't know if I was really attuned to [sexual harassment]—to be quite honest. Maybe that's why I wasn't so aware that it was going on because as a part of my training it had never really been brought up as an issue to be concerned with. (Female Teacher 2)

Another teacher stated, "I don't remember ever specifically talking about sexuality or sexual orientation . . . it was never a specific topic that we were asked to discuss" (Male Teacher 1).

These quotes indicate that teachers are emerging from teacher education programs with no preparation on how to understand and prevent various forms of bullying and gendered harassment. As noted in Chapter 1, forms of gendered harassment are often ignored in bullying research and intervention programs, and this contributes to teachers' inability to intervene in these incidents effectively. These teachers' experiences reflect the findings of other research done with teachers in a school leadership program. In a study conducted in Texas, Stader and Graca (2006) found that 50% of future school administrators reported that in-service training on sexual harassment did not include information on issues related to sexual orientation.

Some of the teachers in my study had taken the initiative to pursue studies that had exposed them to issues of gender, sexual orientation, and race, and they spoke about the importance of these studies in improving their practice as teachers. For example, one teacher spoke about his training as follows:

> I'm not the average teacher or the average individual coming in on the issue. I received a lot of training on gender harassment and bullying and sexual orientation and identities, multiculturalism and racism. All of that was part of my training [as a student leader in university]. . . . I've got the artillery behind me if I want to use it. . . . I've done a lot in the area, compared to a lot of other people. (Male Teacher 1)

The teachers who did get some education in this area are ones who took it upon themselves to seek out these opportunities. Often this motivation to learn was shaped by their internal influences, such as their personal identities and childhood experiences in school.

The perceptions that teachers shared about their experiences with the formal structures of their schools present a clear description of some of the structural obstacles that exist and prevent educators from responding consistently and effectively to incidents of gendered harassment. In addition to structural barriers, teachers also experienced informal barriers to intervention.

Informal Structures: Social Norms

It quickly became apparent that the informal structures of the school, or the social norms and values, exerted the most powerful influence over teachers' behaviors. The three most prevalent themes were (1) perceptions of the administration, (b) interpersonal relationships, and (3) community values. They will be addressed in this order to explore how these factors impacted teachers' experiences in their schools.

Perceptions of the Administration

The first area is teachers' perceptions of their school's administrators. Under this theme, participants spoke about their principal's leadership style, personal values, professional priorities, and policy implementation. The following excerpts demonstrate how the teachers perceived their adminis-trators and how these perceptions shaped their actions in the school.

> Our administrator who dealt with disciplinary problems was a real jock and the real "man's man," and he'd sit the boys down and say, "What the hell do you think you're doing?" I think that he gave them the old football huddle, sit down and I'm gonna tell you how to act in the classroom. And I think that's as far as it went. . . . I feel that the administration didn't want to get involved because they were these [European ethnicity] men and, if they were to come into a staff meeting and say, "We need to address some of the homophobic attitudes," I could never hear them talking about something like that. So maybe that's part of the problem; even the administrators had that [European ethnicity] kind of mentality. (Female Teacher 2)

A second teacher talked about her experiences with administrators as follows:

> I always find that when I'm working with principals and vice principals that it's their own morals and their own beliefs that come through and if it's something that they don't really think is a big issue, then why are they going to be proactive about it? Or just the gender of the administrator, I think that plays into it as well. (Female Teacher 3)

These perceptions demonstrate how powerful an administrator's style is in shaping the culture of a school. Teachers get clear messages from their school leaders about what the administrators personally value and what issues they feel are important to address. Whether it be through official communications in staff meetings, or more typically through observed patterns of behavior and advice from more experienced teachers, a principal's priorities and attitudes toward issues permeate the school and shape the culture. In the case of gen-dered harassment, teachers do not see their administrators making a priority of addressing this problem, and as a result they feel limited in their abilities to change these behavior patterns among students and colleagues.

Another area of administrative influence is that of policy implementa-tion. The way administrators interpreted and applied various school district and schoolwide policies sent clear messages to teachers about how teachers should enforce and apply those policies. Some teachers felt a clear expecta-tion was communicated about bullying policies, whereas others believed that very little had been done to inform teachers about how certain policies should be interpreted and applied. One teacher felt his school had a clear policy on how to address bullying, but he also had the narrowest definition of bullying behaviors. He only viewed acts of physical violence as examples of bullying. He felt as if his school was almost too sensitive to certain acts of covert aggression among students. He explained, "There's no tolerance whatsoever [for bullying] in the school. In fact, in another school, if a kid pulls off another kid's mask [at a Halloween dance], they're not going to get pulled into the principal's office and almost get suspended" (Male Teacher 6).

Other teachers had different perceptions of their school's policies. One spoke about how certain types of harassment are addressed in his school more severely than others:

> The kids are astute enough to see that when they use the word *faggot*, they won't get sent to the office, and when they use a racial slur, they get sent to the office. It's a very quick connection to make. . . . I had one kid call another a faggot. I hauled him to the principal; I asked for a suspension, the principal didn't want to suspend him. It was one of the vice principals and they saw that I was about to blow my top, so they suspended the kid. But I really had to push for it. (Male Teacher 5)

A second teacher talked about the frustration he felt in enforcing school policies when administrators would not support punishments given out by teachers and often bowed to parental pressure if they disagreed with a punishment: "If our hands are tied with enforcement, you can only do so much role modeling"(Male Teacher 1).

In one school, a teacher had worked in an area that had a local anti-bullying law that was enforced by the local police force. He talked about how effective it was as far as raising awareness with posters, community education, and being able to call the police to come and issue a ticket to a student, which he said "helped more people take it seriously" (Male Teacher 7). This discussion shows how teachers emphasize certain rules and policies that have been set out as important to enforce—and as a result, other issues may go unaddressed with students. This tendency to focus on certain policies that are highlighted by the school administrators shows how important it is to have clearly written and consistently enforced policies to address incidents of gender, bullying, and harassment.

The lack of consistency and the lack of clear guidelines or suggestions on how to respond to bullying and harassment left teachers feeling isolated and unsupported in their efforts to address various forms of nonphysical aggression. This lack of support can lead to burnout and reduced efforts in areas of school life that are crucial to student engagement, safety, and success.

Interpersonal Relationships

A second area that was discussed was the role of interpersonal relationships in shaping the school culture. Teachers' personal relationships with their administrators had a significant influence in how they perceived their ability to act in the school. Teachers in two of the four schools did not speak highly of their administrators. One teacher explained that his administrator told him, "If you come out [as a gay man] to those kids, I will not guarantee your safety at this school" (Male Teacher 5). A second teacher described how being a new teacher influenced how she negotiated her relationship with her administrator and led her to handle most bullying incidents on her own. She explained:

> If there's bullying going on in your classroom, then you must be a bad teacher. You don't feel like you can go to [the administration] because it reflects badly upon you as a teacher, because it's like saying to them, "I can't handle my classroom. I need your help." . . . You play the game because the Principal decides what you're going to teach the following year, and if he doesn't like you then he gives you the worst classes and five different subjects to teach and everybody knows it works that way. So if you don't get along with the principal and you don't kiss butt a little bit, then you'll pay for it the next year. That's the power that they have. (Female Teacher 2)

This description of how some principals reward certain teachers and punish others through important decisions such as schedule and workload allocations illustrates how the informal and formal structures of the school interact to shape a teacher's decisions and actions.

The working and personal relationships with colleagues also had an impact on teachers' experiences in their schools. The participants in this study spoke regularly about their struggles and alliances with other members of the school staff. A teacher gave one example of how relationships with new colleagues impacted her actions in the school:

> For the first month, I just do a lot of observing, and I do a lot of talking to teachers, and seeing what's acceptable, what's not, and how we deal with things here at that individual school. So, you're learning everything from the environment. . . . Unfortunately, that's how you pick up bad habits. (Female Teacher 3)

Another teacher expressed his frustration in working against deeply ingrained practices and norms in his school. He was new to the school and was trying to introduce some successful practices he had experienced while working at other schools:

> I'm fighting an uphill battle against inertia. What the school's always done. Some teachers are so resistant to change. That's the kicker, the lack of support from colleagues. We're not helping the kids as much as we could. (Male Teacher 7)

They also expressed frustration about a lack of consistency in enforcing certain school rules and policies. Many felt that they could not defend taking certain actions against students if other teachers were not also addressing those same issues.

> I spent the first couple months enforcing all of this [uniform policy, swearing, and name-calling] and there are some teachers that just never enforce it, and so you realize that out of 20 teachers, we have about 5 who do all the enforcing and you just can't anymore. You can't do it. (Female Teacher 3)

One teacher talked about the inconsistencies in his school and talked through his actions in the classroom by reflecting on the amount of contact he has with each group of students.

> What happens if three other teachers have already had tired days and overlooked the same situation that you're getting? My kids see me 75 minutes 6 days out of 9. A lot of the things I do deal with, I assume that if I see it, it's happening elsewhere, so I need to do something about it. (Male Teacher 1)

As Male Teacher 1 noted, the prevalence of these behaviors is most likely greater than most teachers realize. As another participant pointed out, "There's so much that is completely under the radar of adults" (Male Teacher 8). Since secondary teachers have limited contact with the same group of students during the schoolday, their awareness of the behaviors in a certain group might be limited. The variety of responses by different teachers can impact how students learn about which behaviors are tolerated in school and which ones are not. This lack of consistency can contribute to greater problems with behavior in the school (Mayer, 1995).

The influence of co-workers on teachers who are new to a school cannot be overstated. It is clear that new teachers have to learn the hidden curriculum and unwritten rules of each school they work in. Unfortunately, these informal expectations that get taught in the staff room and through informal interactions often lead to teachers learning bad habits and accepting lower standards of professionalism than they would otherwise set for themselves. Teachers' interactions with and perceptions of their colleagues are also factors that shape how they will act in various situations. A male teacher described an interaction with a colleague where his sexual orientation was called into question when he discussed a date he'd been on using gender-neutral terms. A colleague responded, "As long as it's not with a guy. That would just be weird." He replied, "Why? Why would that be bad?" and "gently put her a little bit on the spot." When reflecting on this interaction, he said,

> I forget how different it is in a "don't ask, don't tell" community. . . .
> This is a woman that I respect a lot, and I was really surprised by that
> reaction. She's considered an open-minded adult in this community,
> and the kids are going to be a couple of steps behind. They're taking
> all of their cues from the adults. (Male Teacher 7)

This interaction demonstrates how more progressive teachers struggle to teach values of acceptance and inclusion to their students when their colleagues, who are respected adults in the community, model behaviors that go against these values.

Two other teachers gave examples of witnessing discriminatory behavior on the basis of race or ethnicity by their colleagues, and these examples illustrate some of the challenges they felt when working against any form of bias in their school. In one example, a teacher of color told about another teacher at his school who was using the word *nigger* regularly in class. In another, a White teacher explained that a student was actually told that "Chinese people aren't creative and so he can't expect to do well on creative assignments" by a member of the teaching staff. Both of these examples were used to illustrate the types of behaviors that were accepted and modeled by colleagues that they felt made it more difficult for them to take action against such behaviors when exhibited by students.

Female Teacher 2 told a more detailed story of an alleged case of sexual harassment by a male colleague toward some female students. Some female students told her that a male teacher was "such a pervert," and Female Teacher 2 discovered through further conversation that he was sexually harassing them. She told the following story about what happened when she tried to report what the students told her:

> I went to the head of my department and spoke to him about it.
> He said, "Yeah, we know, we've spoken to him about it, we see it,
> too." But then it never went to the administrative level. . . . The

administrator and the head of my department happened to be very,
very good friends, so I felt like I don't have a place to go in there. . . .
The new teachers would get upset about things but then they would be
a little bit afraid to go speak to the administration. (Female Teacher 2)

Her frustration and perceived powerlessness in addressing the situation as
a newcomer to the school community was an experience echoed by several
teachers. It is also an example of how more established teachers pass on the
accepted norms, attitudes, and behaviors in the school. As Ormerod, Collinsworth, and Perry (2008) reported in a recent study on sexual harassment
in secondary schools, "School personnel harassing students is an abuse of
power capable of sending a message that harassment will go unpunished
and is thus acceptable" (p. 122). This frustration was also voiced by another
teacher who spoke about the lack of awareness of her more experienced
colleagues and the dismay she felt because they had tenured positions and
would continue to teach and reinforce the status quo at the school:

There's a lot of ignorance. There's a lot of staff that have no idea
about [bullying and harassment]—including myself—no idea how to
deal with [it]. . . . They just don't know how to enforce it. And they
don't know because it doesn't apply to their own personal life. . . .
I just feel like some teachers just don't really have a clue. It's really
scary. It's generally the ones who have been around forever and they
can't do anything with them 'cause they're safe when it comes to
employment. (Female Teacher 3)

Female Teacher 3's statement is supported by findings from other studies
that indicate that more experienced teachers are less sensitive to bullying
and harassment than newer teachers (Borg, 1998) and that male teachers
are less sensitive to covert forms of bullying than female teachers (Ellis &
Shute, 2007). The stories that these teachers shared about the frustration
they felt and the difficulties they faced due to colleagues who acted in irre-
sponsible or oppressive ways were troubling. It is not surprising to see how
challenging it is to work against various forms of bias and harassment when
professional educators and employees of the school are modeling the exact
behaviors these teachers are trying to prevent.

Teachers' relationships with students and parents also had an influence
on their responses to various forms of bullying and harassment. The participants in this study spoke mostly of a high respect and a deep level of care for
their students and their overall well-being. They also emphasized the importance of being consistent and establishing clear expectations and boundaries
for student behavior. They spoke about avoiding power struggles by setting

up clear expectations and working to develop a strong rapport with their students by interacting with them as individuals and outside the classroom setting. One gay teacher explained that he chose to remain closeted to protect his students from the potential discomfort of learning that a favored teacher is gay—something they've been taught by their religion is wrong.

They also articulated the struggles they faced in trying to deal effectively with bullying. They worked very hard to have positive relationships with their students—often making themselves available during their own free time to provide homework assistance and extracurricular supervision or opening up their classrooms for students to hang out in during lunch periods. They felt that these extra efforts made them more approachable than other teachers and allowed them to develop more meaningful connections with certain students so that they could provide them additional support. Several teachers spoke of special relationships with certain students that had resulted from these extra efforts. It was clear that these connections were quite meaningful to the teachers and very likely had a significant positive impact on the students and their perceptions of and experiences in their school community.

Teachers' perceptions and responses were also influenced by interactions with parents. This was not a prevalent theme through all teachers' experiences, but the teachers who did address the issue of parent interactions indicated that it had an impact on how they felt they were able to address certain behaviors in the school. The teachers gave several examples of the challenges of working with parents around issues of discipline and harassment. One teacher talked about being targeted for homophobic harassment by parents in the community. He explained, "I was getting called faggot and parents were calling, were coming onto the property to harass me while I was doing yard duty" (Male Teacher 5). Another teacher spoke of his challenges dealing with parents:

> There's a different culture now with parents not backing up the behavior, or a student that you're punishing for a certain word that they used in class and then the father comes into the school for a meeting and says, "Well, what the f——k are you doing suspending my son?" (Male Teacher 1)

These examples show that the study participants feel that parents are often working against what they are trying to accomplish with students. Whether it is modeling disrespectful behavior toward teachers, targeting them for harassment, or flaunting the rules of the school, these parental behaviors often actively work against the possibility of reducing gendered harassment in school. It seems evident that the accumulation of these interactions with administrators, colleagues, students, and parents conveys clear and consistent messages to teachers about which behaviors are tolerated in a school and which ones are not. These social norms do not emerge in a vacuum; rather, they are often a reflection of the community in which the school is located.

School Community

The schools in this study were situated in very different communities. The dominant cultural group and socioeconomic status of the students in the school communities varied greatly. Teachers in two schools described their schools as having mostly White, middle-class, privileged students. One of these schools was dominated by a specific European ethnic group that fostered a culture of male dominance. One teacher from this school explained:

> My [European ethnicity] boys had such big egos, and they thought that they should be waited on by their teachers, [and] by their fellow girl students. They thought they were really, really important and they were obviously led to believe that by their families. (Female Teacher 2)

Teachers in a third school talked about the multiple oppressions the majority of their students face due to the challenges of being new immigrants and the daily realities of poverty and ethnic conflicts in the community. This school had a difficult relationship with the community it was in. The students were visibly different from the dominant ethno-cultural group in the area and were often blamed for any disruptions or damage in the area. The teachers stated that the police visited the school regularly to respond to issues of school violence and complaints from the community.

Teachers in a fourth school described the value of being "rednecky" and good at sports in their working-class farming community. In this school, being a redneck was a source of pride. For example, the brand of tractor students had on their farm was a status symbol. One teacher gave the example of a student who had been targeted with anti-gay insults. He explained why he thought this was so: "Just because he's not rednecky. He doesn't go out of his way to be a tough person" (Male Teacher 8). In all the conversations with these teachers, it was clear that the values and expectations of the community were significant factors that shaped what could and could not happen in their schools. Their interpersonal relationships with colleagues and families were created in this context and often actively transmitted the values of the broader school community. These, in turn, influenced the school culture. Although these four schools had markedly different student populations and were in different types of communities, all the teachers expressed the feeling that gendered harassment was prevalent and that macho values expressed through heterosexual harassment and homophobic name-calling were endemic to their schools.

Although the teachers made some broad generalizations in their descriptions of the school communities, these generalizations give us an understanding of how the teachers framed their experiences with their students. Educators rarely have the luxury of working with students as individuals and often construct lessons and interactions based on what they know about their students as a group. Teachers saw how external influences from students' families, community values, and out-of-school time played a role in shaping the climate and priorities of the school. Although all of these schools had very different cultures and social realities, the participants spoke of very similar obstacles to addressing forms of gendered harassment.

CONCLUSION

External influences, both formal and informal, interact with teachers' own experiences and philosophies to shape how they choose to act when confronted with bullying and harassment in school. As previous researchers have found, school culture is much more likely than official policies and procedures to determine what it is that students, teachers, and administrators say and do. This means that teachers are more inclined to act in ways that reflect shared norms and values of other teachers than in ways defined by school policy (Stader & Graca, 2006). Teachers' internal influences— such as their educational philosophy, personal identities, and own experiences in school—also have an impact on how they perceive and respond to incidents of bullying and harassment in school. The next chapter offers an explanation of the internal influences of the teachers in this study.

CHAPTER 4

Who We Are Matters: Teachers' Responses to Bullying and Harassment

I think about the times when I got called "fag." They're the most poignant memories of my high school and elementary career. I made sure my students knew I didn't tolerate any of that stuff.

—Male Teacher 5

When examining any aspect of school culture, it is important to recognize that individuals work together, consciously and unconsciously, to create and perpetuate this culture. Teachers are the individuals who are responsible for representing and communicating the school's expectations to students and family members. They do this by teaching the formal curriculum, enforcing official policies, and modeling behavioral norms as well as by facilitating extracurricular activities and communicating with students, parents, colleagues, and administration. Although the culture of the school is dynamic and cannot be changed by a single individual, teachers play a pivotal role in either perpetuating or transforming a school's culture. As a result, it is important to understand the factors that shape how teachers experience their schools' culture as well as the barriers and motivators they describe as influencing their actions in response to incidents of gendered harassment.

Each individual brings a specific set of identities and life experiences to school. What quickly became clear in interviews with teachers were four main influences that shaped how they perceived the culture of their current school: teaching philosophy, educational biography, life experiences, and identities. This chapter provides detailed descriptions of the different internal influences described by the teachers in this research and how these impacted their perceptions of and responses to bullying and harassment. These identities were discussed and explored through the series of three life-history interviews that were conducted by the author with each teacher as part of this research. (For more information on the structure and content of these inteviews, please see Meyer, 2008b, and in press.)

INTERNAL INFLUENCES

Teaching Philosophy

The way in which teachers talked about their roles and responsibilities in the classroom provided a way of understanding their philosophy of teaching. This clearly shaped the way they interacted with their students. The teachers who volunteered to participate in this study all expressed a holistic view of their role in the classroom. They viewed their responsibilities as extending far beyond teaching their assigned courses and expressed a commitment to issues of lifelong learning, citizenship, and social justice. One teacher explained how she perceived her role in the classroom as follows:

> I would place more of an emphasis on my job as a role model in the classroom than I would on all of those other little tasks that come along with the teaching profession. I would say my job is to teach students and to help them become lifelong learners. To teach them a process of learning, but also to teach them about the type of people they want to be, the type of citizens they want to be in their communities. How they want to relate to other people. (Female Teacher 2)

Other teachers echoed this sentiment of being a mentor and a role model and making students aware of broader social issues and important life skills. A second teacher described his content area as a vehicle for what he considered his main responsibilities in the classroom: "Science is totally a tool for me to help them grow as people. Its one of the reasons I switched to middle school, because I could help them with my real goal, which is helping them be good citizens" (Male Teacher 7). These are examples of the way the teachers described their role in schools. They clearly placed a higher priority on modeling good citizenship and supporting individual students over teaching their assigned curricular content.

A third teacher explained that he worked to integrate current events and important social issues in his class discussions by talking about events in the news and addressing stereotypes and assumptions in students' language and behavior: "I'm only obliged to teach the content, but as a teacher . . . you can't help but impart values upon your students" (Male Teacher 1). These teachers had constructed a professional philosophy that allowed them to meet their personal objectives as well as satisfy their professional obligations. A teaching philosophy that included an emphasis on teaching broader social skills beyond the subject matter was one of the clear motivators that encouraged teachers to intervene in incidents of bullying and gendered harassment.

Educational Biography

The second important source of internal influences was the teachers' own school experiences as students. Their educational biographies clearly shaped how they perceived and responded to forms of bullying and harassment in their classrooms. When talking about bullying and harassment, teachers often reflected on their experiences as children in school and at home. They spoke of their own memories of sexism, racism, and homophobia as well as how these experiences strongly influenced their teaching philosophy and how they handled issues with their students. Many of them identified their own painful memories of school as central in motivating them to go into teaching. One teacher recalled his school experiences and how they impacted his current teaching practice: "Being a gay man, having experienced harassment, made me define my role as a teacher" (Male Teacher 5). Another teacher recounted his memories of being the only visible minority in his school as follows:

> I got incredibly bullied. I was called everything: Black, Jew, and
> Vietnamese. I got into fights every single day. When I started teaching,
> I started remembering all those horrible things. I have to tell the other
> kids: "Stop using those words—they're hurtful." (Male Teacher 6)

These early-childhood experiences clearly made most of the teachers in this study more sensitive to the harmful impacts of bullying and harassment. They talked about the long-term effects these memories had on how they interact with students and colleagues in their current positions. Other teachers described the difficult memories of "having someone as your best friend and the next day you're enemies" (Female Teacher 3). These early painful experiences in schools were also important motivators for teachers to intervene in cases of bullying and harassment.

Life Experiences

A third factor that influenced teachers was their own life experiences outside of school. This theme includes other personal and professional experiences that teachers spoke about as having an impact on how they perceive and respond to bullying and harassment. The most common topic in this category was teachers' own experiences with discrimination and harassment. This was related to their educational biographies but generally included out-of-school childhood memories as well as more recent personal and professional interactions. For example, teachers spoke about how long they had been working in a certain community as impacting how comfortable they felt addressing more controversial issues such as homophobia or sexual harassment. Female Teacher 2 talked about her reluctance to address homophobia in a school run by more conservative administrators by saying, "You worry until your job is secure."

Another teacher described how his interactions with a student who came out at his school had an impact on his own attitudes toward homosexuality. He had stated in one of his interviews that "I don't necessarily agree with homosexuality" but that he was conscious of his use of expressions such as "that's so gay" and was trying to correct himself. One year after the interviews, I shared some of my preliminary findings with the teachers, and Male Teacher 6 wrote back by saying,

> I know I said that, but at the same time I don't feel it reflects my view on the matter. I would prefer to say that homosexuality does not make anyone less of a person. My student who was openly gay and a recent documentary on homosexuality have really helped me in my views on this topic.

Male Teacher 6's recent experiences had an impact on his views and were causing him to shift his attitudes toward homosexuality. This is a good example of the potential positive impact of educational interventions that provide more information and interaction with individuals on issues such as sexual orientation and gender identity.

Teachers who identified as gay or bisexual talked about their own experiences with discrimination. One teacher was targeted by colleagues for persistent and severe sexual orientation harassment that caused him to take sick leave and eventually to leave the school. These experiences made him more sensitive to acts of sexual orientation harassment but also made him feel vulnerable. This vulnerability was expressed as a hesitancy to address anti-gay incidents as much as he would like. Both teachers of color who participated in this study talked about their own experiences with racism and spoke about how this increased their sensitivity to racial harassment and other forms of institutional racism. These life experiences were closely connected to important parts of the teachers' identities that they spoke about when reflecting on the issues of bullying and harassment in their schools.

Identities

In their interviews, teachers spoke most regularly about the aspects of themselves that had been marginalized in the dominant culture or had been targeted for discrimination in their educational biographies and life experiences. Teachers would preface certain comments with statements like "as a woman" or "as a gay man" to indicate that that aspect of their identity was central to how they were experiencing and responding to certain situations. One teacher asked aloud, "Am I more vigilant because I'm gay?" and answered himself by saying, "Probably. But it's the right thing to do" (Male Teacher 1). A second teacher reflected on her feelings of vulnerability as a bisexual woman trying to address homophobia in her school: "I'm vulnerable. When you yourself are gay, you're even more scared. You think you're going to be attacked. You know it's going to be personal. I'm sensitive to more than your average teacher" (Female Teacher 3). A third teacher echoed this sensitivity by explaining:

> It's tough as a teacher of color. I have to be very careful. It really hits me personally. It's hard not to let my emotions get all tangled up in there. I have very little room to slip up. Is this because I am a woman of color? Is that really about race? Yeah, maybe. (Female Teacher 4)

It is interesting to note that the two participants in the study who identified as White, heterosexual males never explicitly spoke about their race, gender, or sexual orientation, whereas all the other teachers did. This may indicate that individuals who have not personally experienced forms of social oppression such as racism, sexism, or homophobia may have more difficulty learning to see and understand forms of bias in the school and society as a whole. This brings us to a discussion of how teachers' internal influences impact their perceptions of and responses to bullying and harassment.

IMPACTS OF INTERNAL INFLUENCES ON TEACHERS' PERCEPTIONS AND RESPONSES

These four internal influences had a strong impact on teachers' levels of awareness of various forms of bullying and harassment. The White, heterosexual male teachers were more likely to speak in general terms about bullying, whereas the gay and bisexual teachers spoke at great length about homophobia and sexual orientation harassment. The teachers of color gave more examples and detailed descriptions of racial and ethnic forms of harassment, and female participants tended to provide more information and detail about incidents of heterosexual harassment. Participants spoke only briefly about harassment for gender nonconformity, although it often came up as a reason for why a student was being targeted with sexual orientation harassment. A similar finding was reported by James Ryan in his study on perceptions of racism by school administrators. He reported that most administrators "generally equate racism with individual acts on the part of people who they believe are malicious, ignorant, or not capable of exercising good judgment"(Ryan, 2003, p. 150), and they therefore reported extremely low rates of racism in their schools. He explains that most white administrators could not "see" the racism due to their White privilege. Ryan (2003) goes on to assert that "those who are the objects of oppression are often better able to gain insight into the manner in which they are oppressed than those who are not, or those who, however unwittingly, are part of that system of oppression" (p. 155). This standpoint theory has also been advanced by other feminist, anti-racist, and anti-oppressive scholars (Hartsock, 1993/1997; McIntosh, 1988/2004; Young, 1990).

Although the conclusion that individuals are more sensitive to experiences that they have lived themselves might seem obvious, the implications are more complex: How do we educate teachers to see patterns of behavior that they haven't already been taught to understand from personal experience? Is it possible to teach members of a dominant group to see and understand the marginalization and discrimination experienced by a targeted group? I believe it is possible, but only if a commitment is made by teacher education and school leadership programs. This is an important challenge that pre-service and in-service teacher and administrator education programs must address.

Although the teachers did not have the same degree of sensitivity to these various forms of bullying and harassment, most of the teachers in this study spoke of their personal desire or commitment to challenge gendered harassment in their schools. In spite of this personal commitment, they felt limited in their actions by a perceived lack of support from the administration and/or their colleagues. They also reported feeling isolated in addressing the problem of homophobic name-calling in particular, stating that it was too prevalent an issue in their school for them to tackle alone. The lack of intervention by colleagues and the lack of demonstrated support from the administration resulted in many of these teachers giving up and limiting their interventions to only the most severe offenses. The lack of consistency in reporting and response to such incidents among colleagues and the lack of a clear policy and definitions to guide teachers in the classrooms and hallways were significant obstacles these teachers faced in their school cultures.

In spite of these obstacles, many of the teachers gave detailed examples of how they attempted to address incidents of gendered harassment when they witnessed it. The most consistent response that teachers described was to turn an incident into a teachable moment. This reflects the "stop and educate" model advocated by the Gay, Lesbian, and Straight Education Network (GLSEN) (Goldstein, 2001). This model encourages educators to "stop" any harmful name-calling behavior when they observe it and then "educate" the individuals involved either publicly or privately. This model allows teachers to establish a consistent yet flexible response to such incidents. It also encourages them to provide students with more information about why certain terms, phrases, and "jokes" are hurtful and not appropriate in school. Fostering dialogue and offering more information about certain "jokes," comments, and insults are essential for students to understand the implications of their behaviors and take steps to change them.

A second approach teachers have taken is to dedicate a full class session early in the schoolyear to addressing name-calling as well as other forms of bullying and harassment. Unfortunately, one teacher in this study experienced backlash from his administration after spending class time on these topics. He was told that because he was a French teacher and issues of racism, sexism, and homophobia were not part of his curriculum, he should not be spending instructional time addressing these issues. This is another example of how administrators' actions send strong messages to teachers about which actions are endorsed by the school culture and which are not.

Most participants spoke of the importance of being consistent and setting up clear expectations at the beginning of the schoolyear. Although they noted that their colleagues usually did not support attempts to reduce sexual and sexual orientation harassment, the teachers reported that by being clear and consistent, they could still have an influence on the behavior in their classrooms.

Another teacher gave an example of authentic consequences that involve the entire class. In this situation, there was graffiti on a table that said "_____ is a homo." She used this as an opportunity to talk to her students about why this term was inappropriate and then had everyone spend the period cleaning all graffiti off the desks and tables in her classroom. These are just a few examples from the research participants that offer some suggestions for teachers to apply in their classrooms. Chapter 6 will provide more detailed examples of individual and whole-school responses to help reduce gendered harassment.

CONCLUSION

The teachers in this study viewed themselves as different from the average educator. They generally described themselves as more educated, more aware, and more sensitive to issues of gender, race, ethnicity, and sexual orientation as well as related forms of bias, discrimination, bullying, and harassment. Every single participant spoke of a personal commitment to challenging bullying and harassment. This was often paired with an articulation of a marginalized aspect of their own identity: woman, gay, or ethnic minority. Most of these teachers had a political consciousness about social inequalities that had been shaped by their own educational biographies, life experiences, and identities. This consciousness influenced their teaching philosophies and how they perceived their students and school cultures. They were articulate in critiquing issues regarding the policies and administration of the school and the impacts of other external factors that influenced students' experiences in their schools.

These findings offer us a deeper understanding of how various forms of bullying and harassment are perceived by teachers who may be more sensitive to them than are other educators. With their increased sensitivity, these teachers can be seen as canaries in the coal mine sounding the alarm about the hazards that exist in current school cultures. These data can offer scholars, educators, and school leaders a clearer picture of some of the challenges that exist when trying to confront such behaviors in schools.

Successful bullying and violence intervention programs require consistent implementation, which in turn requires securing the support of the entire professional staff of the school. In order to establish this level of support, one must understand the individuals who are responsible for carrying out the program. To achieve this understanding, there must be more of a focus on identity work in teacher education and school leadership programs and more discussions about the impacts that identities can have in shaping educators' own philosophies and approaches to working with students. It is essential for educators to recognize the influence of their own educational biographies, life experiences, and personal identities and how these impact how they interact with their students and colleagues. We learn stereotypes and biases through our education and upbringing. If we never get a chance to identify and unlearn the harmful ones, then they will continue to impact everyone around us.

As several teachers pointed out, it was their personal experiences with discrimination and marginalization that made them particularly sensitive to these issues in schools. The challenge that these findings present is how to raise the awareness of educators who have not personally felt the impacts of discrimination or exclusion from dominant culture as well as how to retain passionate and critically thinking educators when certain school cultures seem intent on forcing them out. It is clearly a challenge to maintain a teaching identity that is progressive and transformative while working within an institution that is designed to maintain and pass on dominant values. Deborah Britzman talks about this problem in *Practice Makes Practice: A Critical Study of Learning to Teach* (2003). She writes about the challenges facing student teachers when they enter their own classrooms:

> Once student teachers are severed from the social context of teaching, the compulsion is to reproduce rather than transform their institutional biography. The values embedded in the institutional biography become sedimented, and serve as the foundation for the uneasy acceptance of cultural myths that legitimize and render as natural the hierarchical views of authority, knowledge, and power. (p. 236)

This overreliance on the norms of the institution to guide their practice can cause educators to become jaded, apathetic, and ineffective. In order to work in the best interests of their students, teachers must be supported in retaining their own identities and perspectives. By maintaining a critical view of their own school communities, educators can more readily respond to the needs of targeted students and help support the school community to continually adapt and renew itself. At the same time, institutions must be guided by legal and ethical polices and practices to ensure that students are being given equal educational opportunities and access to public services. The next chapter outlines important legal standards and precedents that exist to help individuals and institutions better understand their legal obligations to protect students in schools from gendered harassment.

CHAPTER 5

What Educators Need to Know About the Law

Many educators are unaware of the legal guidelines that currently exist to protect students from experiencing forms of gendered harassment in schools. This lack of knowledge often exposes students to a hostile school climate. This ignorance also exposes teachers, administrators, and school board personnel to legal and financial liability in cases of peer harassment. Moreover, understanding the legal issues that are involved in cases of harassment can help empower educators to take appropriate steps to advocate for students and actively work to improve their school environments. This chapter provides several case studies and an overview of the relevant federal and state laws that are applicable in each scenario. This format offers an accessible guide to understanding key legal issues and how to effectively intervene in cases of gendered harassment in the context of existing legal precedents.

In the United States several legal protections exist for students experiencing gendered harassment in their schools. At the federal level, lawyers have successfully applied Title IX and Equal Protection in such cases. In addition to these federal protections, a range of state and local nondiscrimination laws may also apply. Each of these laws and the elements that apply to teachers and administrators will be explained through the case studies in this chapter.

Most educators want what is best for all of their students. However, educators can often be overwhelmed by the multiple demands placed on them to meet established curriculum standards, have their students score well on high-stakes tests, and accomplish this with limited time and funding. When there seem to be competing demands for limited class time and resources, the law can provide a clear framework of expectations for school leaders and educational staff. Law and policy can also be powerful educational tools to help teachers and school leaders acknowledge the significance of gendered harassment, which is often ignored and minimized in schools. Finally, the existing case law provides some valuable guidelines that can help reduce school liability if teachers, administrators, and school board personnel consistently apply the lessons learned from the cases discussed in this chapter.

School staff need more guidance on how to proactively address cases of gendered harassment in schools. For the purposes of this discussion, school staff refers to all adult representatives of the school district, from volunteers to the governing board. This includes support staff (such as bus drivers, cafeteria personnel, monitors, office staff, and parent volunteers), educational and health professionals (pedagogical consultants, classroom teachers, para-educators or aides, librarians, school counselors, nurses, and coaches), and school leaders (vice principals, principals, and superintendents).

CASE STUDY: SEXUAL HARASSMENT

Case One: Lashonda Davis

In the fifth grade, a male classmate of LaShonda's tried to touch her breasts and told her, "I want to get in bed with you" and "I want to feel your boobs." She reported this to her mother and teacher, but the school didn't do anything to support LaShonda or punish the perpetrator. This harassment continued: verbal taunts, leers in class, and unwanted behaviors. Gym class was the worst. One time he put a door stop in his pants and walked up to her, thrusting his crotch. Another time he rubbed his body up against LaShonda in the school hallway. LaShonda reported each of these incidents to her teachers but still had to sit next to this student in class, and nothing was done to get the harassment to stop.

The incidents stopped 6 months later when her parents decided to charge him with sexual battery. He pled guilty to this charge. During this time, LaShonda's previously high grades had dropped, and her father discovered that she had written a suicide note *(Davis v. Monroe County Board of Education, 1999)*.

These events led to a landmark Supreme Court decision that applied Title IX of the 1972 Educational Amendments to cases of student-on-student sexual harassment. Although Title IX is most widely known for its impact in reducing disparities between men and women in athletic participation at the collegiate level, it was written to protect individuals from being denied educational benefits on the basis of sex (Roth, 1994). It was first successfully applied in the context of a sexual harassment claim in the case of *Franklin v. Gwinett County Public Schools* (1992). This Supreme Court decision set the precedent for using Title IX to defend students from harassment based on sex, but in this case the defendant was a school board employee (Roth,

1994). The facts of LaShonda Davis's case presented here provide a way to understand where the school failed to take appropriate action to protect LaShonda from the persistent, pervasive, and severe harassment she was experiencing from a peer in her fifth-grade classroom.

In cases of sexual harassment such as this one, there are four main criteria that must be met under the application of Title IX (*Davis v. Monroe County Board of Education,* 1999):

1. School officials have *actual knowledge* of the harassment.
2. School officials demonstrate *deliberate indifference* to harassment or take actions that are *clearly unreasonable.*
3. School officials have substantial control over both the harasser and the context in which the known harassment occurs.
4. The harassment is so *severe, pervasive and objectively offensive* that it can be said to *deprive the victim(s) of access* to the educational opportunities or benefits provided by the school.

In this case, LaShonda Davis and her parents had repeatedly notified her teacher and the principal of the harassment she was experiencing over a 5-month period. The family alleged that the school did nothing in response. One teacher even refused to allow LaShonda to change her seat, so she was forced to sit next to her harasser in class every day (Rollini, 2003). The school also lacked a harassment policy that would have provided LaShonda and her family an avenue to work with the school to correct the situation. This combination of *actual knowledge* and acts of *deliberate indifference* is essential in harassment cases under Title IX. The Office for Civil Rights (OCR) clarifies that it does not make schools responsible for the actions of the harassing student, "but rather for its own discrimination in failing to take immediate and appropriate steps to remedy the hostile environment once a school official knows about it"(OCR, 1997). Finally, it is also important to note that in cases decided in favor of the student, federally funded institutions may be held financially liable for damages (Rollini, 2003).

Although Title IX and the OCR provide clear guidelines and protections for students experiencing sexual harassment, legal scholar Gigi Rollini (2003) argues that "the only victims that succeed under *Davis* are ones that are utterly debilitated by the harassment" (p. 995). This is due to the fourth criterion, which requires students to demonstrate that the harassment was so severe that it deprived them of access to an education. This shields the legal system from having to handle minor complaints; however, it provides minimal protection to students who are experiencing harassment but manage to maintain their academic performance in spite of it. Educators need to take all complaints of gendered harassment seriously and take appropriate steps to ensure that it stops—not wait for there to be measurable impacts on students' school performance and physical or mental health to take action. In addition to protecting students from heterosexual harassment, Title IX has also been used to defend the rights of students who have been targeted for sexual orientation harassment.

CASE STUDIES: SEXUAL ORIENTATION HARASSMENT

Case Two: Derek Henkle

When he was in the ninth grade, Derek Henkle came out at his Reno, Nevada, public school. Almost immediately, he was harassed about his sexual orientation. On one occasion, students lassoed him around his neck in the school parking lot and threatened to kill him by dragging him from their truck. Instead of dealing with his attackers and ensuring his safety, school authorities treated Henkle as if he were the problem and transferred him to an alternative school for troubled students. The principal there told Henkle to "stop acting like a fag." After a transfer to yet a third school, Henkle was beaten bloody by another student while two school security guards stood by. Unwilling to take measures to create a safe educational environment for Henkle, school officials had him take classes at a local community college to obtain a GED instead of a high school diploma (*Henkle v. Gregory*, 2001).

There are currently no federal protections that specifically protect lesbian, gay, bisexual, and transgendered (LGBT) people from discrimination in the United States. In legal terms, they are not considered a suspect or quasi-suspect class, which means in the U.S. they are not specifically protected from discrimination at the federal level. However, sexual minorities are entitled to the same protection as any other identifiable group (*Beall v. London City School District*, 2006; *Romer v. Evans*, 1996). Consequently, a variety of courts across the country have begun holding school districts liable for their failure to adequately address student-on-student harassment and bullying based on real or perceived sexual orientation. Due to the lack of explicit protections, the success of these cases depends on the courts' interpretations and the lawyers' arguments based on existing protections. Derek Henkle's case is one of several cases that have successfully made the argument that Title IX can also protect students from peer sexual orientation harassment.

The case *Henkle v. Gregory* (2001) provides one example of how a student's complaint led to far-reaching changes in his school district and the extension of legal protections to GLBT youth. In this case, the federal district court of Nevada allowed the Title IX sexual orientation harassment of Derek Henkle for punitive damages to proceed. The school district chose to settle this case and awarded $451,000 in damages to the student. Part of the settlement included changes to several district policies on discrimination and harassment to include sexual orientation and gender expression. This case also established students' right to be out at school by extending existing First Amendment protections for free speech to student expression about their sexual orientation (Lambda Legal, 2001). Although the First Amendment issues of this case are important to understand, they are beyond the scope of this chapter. However, it is important to note that the school may not limit student expression unless it can show that it will "materially and substantially interfere with the requirements of appropriate discipline in the operation of the school" (*Tinker v. Des Moines Independent School District*, 1969).

In a similar case, a California federal district court concluded:

> the Court finds no material difference between the instance in which a female student is subject to unwelcome sexual comments and advances due to her harasser's perception that she is a sex object, and the instance in which a male student is insulted and abused due to his harasser's perception that he is a homosexual, and therefore a subject of prey. In both instances, the conduct is a heinous response to the harasser's perception of the victim's sexuality, and is not distinguishable to this court. (*Ray v. Antioch Unified School District*, 2000, p. 1170)

In *Ray v. Antioch Unified School District* (2000), and *Montgomery v. Independent School District* (2000), separate federal district courts (California and Minnesota, respectively) decided that schools could be held liable under Title IX for acting with "deliberate indifference" toward students who have reported persistent and severe sexual orientation harassment at school. These decisions applied the four criteria established in *Davis v. Monroe County Board of Education* (1999) described earlier, and held that Title IX could be effectively used to defend students in cases of sexual orientation harassment by their peers.

The Equal Protection Clause of the Fourteenth Amendment is another avenue for relief for students experiencing gendered harassment in school, as demonstrated in the next case.

Case Three: Jamie Nabozny

Starting in eighth grade, Jamie was tormented in school. For 3 years he was targeted for anti-gay harassment after he had come out. At school, he was urinated on, "mock raped," and beaten to the point of hospitalization. He reported these incidents repeatedly to school administrators, but the perpetrators were never punished and the harassment never abated. At one point, the principal told him that he should expect such treatment if he was going to be openly gay. Jamie quit school twice and attempted suicide on two different occasions as a result of this harassment (*Nabozny v. Podlesny*, 1996).

Jamie Nabozny's case against his school administrators was won based on the Fourteenth Amendment's Equal Protection Clause, which states that, "no State shall . . . deny to any person within its jurisdiction the equal protection of the laws" (Section 1). In order to establish liability under sec. 1983 of title 42 of the United States Code, Nabozny had to prove three facts:

1. That the defendants acted with nefarious discriminatory purpose
2. That they discriminated against him based on his membership in a definable class
3. That the administrators acted either intentionally or with deliberate indifference (*Nabozny v. Podlesny*, 1996, p. 5)

The Seventh Circuit Court of Appeals found that the school administrators were liable for violating Nabozny's Fourteenth Amendment right of equal protection. In this case, Nabozny's lawyers demonstrated that he was treated differently from other students and that this treatment was based on his sex and sexual orientation. A major deciding factor in this was the school's response to the mock rape. The court wrote, "We find it impossible to believe that a female lodging a similar complaint would have received the same response" (p. 5). One way that defendants can protect themselves from liability in such cases is to present a "rational basis" for their conduct. In this case the court stated, "We are unable to garner any rational bases for permitting one student to assault another based on the victim's sexual orientation, and the defendants do not offer us one" (p. 12). Before a jury could decide on damages, an out-of-court settlement of $900,000 was agreed upon by both parties. In this case, the administrators were held personally liable because the school district had anti-harassment policies in place that protected it from legal liability. This case was the first time that federal law was held to apply to anti-gay discrimination in schools and set a high price tag on allowing peer-to-peer harassment to be ignored in schools (Lipkin, 1999). One other example of youth pursuing action against their school using the equal protection argument was in the case *Flores v. Morgan Hill* (2003).

Case Four: Alana Flores

Throughout her years in high school, students placed pages torn from pornographic magazines in Alana's locker and scratched anti-gay obscenities into the paint on her locker door. Although she reported it, the school left the words on her locker for months before painting over them. In January of 1997, Alana found a picture of a naked woman, bound and gagged, with her legs spread and her throat slashed taped to her locker. On the picture, someone had written, "Die, die, Dyke bitch, fuck off. We'll kill you." Alana, frightened and crying, took the photo to the assistant principal's office. The assistant principal brushed her off and told her to go back to class, saying, "Don't bring me this trash anymore; this is disgusting." The assistant principal then asked Alana if she was gay and said, "If you're not gay, why are you crying?"(ACLU, 2004, p. 1).

The Equal Protection Clause of the Fourteenth Amendment guarantees equal application of a law to all people in the United States (Macgillivray, 2007). As mentioned above, an equal protection claim requires the student to show that school officials: (1) *did not fairly and consistently apply policies* when dealing with the student; (2) were *deliberately indifferent* to the student's complaints, or treated the student in a manner that was (3) *clearly unreasonable* (Stader, 2007). In *Flores v. Morgan Hill* (2003), the federal Ninth Circuit Court of Appeals found ample evidence of deliberate indifference to the ongoing sexual orientation harassment of six students in this California school district and decided in favor of the students. The students proved that the school district "discriminated against them as members of an identifiable class and that the discrimination was intentional" (*Flores v. Morgan Hill,* 2003, p. 4780). This decision resulted in a $1,100,000 settlement being awarded to the students (ACLU, 2004) and the requirement that the school district implement a training and education program for its administrators, faculty, and students (Dignan, 2004).

The settlement agreement for this case can be a valuable guide for schools looking to improve their school climate and reduce acts of gendered harassment and will be presented at length at the end of the chapter along with other recommendations from these case studies.

CASE STUDIES: HARASSMENT FOR GENDER NONCONFORMITY

Case Five: John Doe

John Doe and his parents filed suit against the Bellefonte Area School District for being "deliberately indifferent" to 3 years of peer sexual harassment Doe encountered on account of his effeminate characteristics. He was teased, called homophobic insults, threatened, intimidated, and assaulted by his fellow students at school. This ongoing harassment prevented Doe from participating in extracurricular activities, and his grades were adversely affected (*Doe v. Bellefonte Area School District,* 2004; "Student May Sue School," 2003).

The case of *Doe v. Bellefonte School District* is a helpful one to examine for two reasons. First, it explicitly addresses the issue of students targeting another student for harassment based on gender nonconforming behaviors. Second, it can act as a model for school districts on how to respond, as the outcome of this case was decided in the school's favor. Doe and his lawyers argued that the school's response to his ongoing harassment was "deliberately indifferent" because the school's response was not 100% effective in stemming the harassment. In examining the facts of the case, the court wanted to determine if the actions of the district in response to Doe's allegations were "clearly unreasonable."

What the court learned is that the school responded to Doe's harassers in the following ways: (1) Each time he complained, the school responded with "reasonable actions that eliminated further harassment" of Doe by that particular student; (2) students were suspended, given warnings, and counseled on the seriousness of harassment; (3) the school district sent memos to faculty and staff informing them of Doe's harassment and requesting assistance to prevent further incidents; (4) Doe was provided with a "special means" of reporting harassment directly to the school psychologist; and (5) the school held assemblies and enacted policies addressing peer-to-peer harassment *(Doe v. Bellefonte Area School District*, 2004). This list of varied and appropriate responses led the U.S. Court of Appeals for the Third Circuit to support the district court's decision in favor of the school district. Therefore, schools that may find themselves subject to similar complaints could reduce their legal liability and improve student safety by applying a multitiered response as demonstrated by the actions of the Bellefonte Area School District.

Montgomery v. Independent School Dist. No. 709 (2000) also addressed the issue of a student being targeted and harassed for exhibiting gender nonconforming behavior; however, this case was decided in favor of the student. In *Montgomery,* the court found that Title IX damages could be awarded to students on the basis of sexual orientation harassment, since such harassment is often based on a "failure to meet expected gender stereotypes" (p. 1091). Montgomery's case was settled for an undisclosed financial amount (Skowronski, 2008).

Case Six: Pat Doe

In 2000, Pat was a student in the seventh grade at a school in Massachusetts and often wore clothing and fashion accessories typically worn by girls. This caused great difficulty for Pat because she was born biologically male. During seventh and eighth grade, Pat was repeatedly sent home from school by the principal when her outfits were too "girl-like." By the time Pat was in eighth grade, the principal had asked Pat to check with him to have her clothing approved on a daily basis and often sent her home. Pat eventually stopped attending school as a result of the hostility she faced there (*Doe v. Brockton Sch. Comm.*, 2000).

This case is important to discuss because it is the only legal decision found in the research for this book that addresses the realities faced by transgender youth in schools. Although the court's decision was grounded in local legal protections, the arguments advanced and the outcome are of interest to those working to improve student safety and gender equity in schools.

The Commonwealth of Massachusetts Appeals Court found that the treatment Pat Doe received from her school principal violated sex discrimination protections provided by the commonwealth and that the school could not place restrictions on her attire based on her sex assigned at birth. In this case, Doe's lawyers based their arguments about student expression and gender identity on cases such as *Tinker v. Des Moines Independent School District* (1969), a landmark case that established guidelines for the application of First Amendment protections for student expression in school, and *Montgomery v. Independent School District* (2000), described above, to defend her right to attend school dressed in typically feminine attire, including makeup, jewelry, bras, and long hair. The appeals court supported the lower court's decision to issue an injunction requiring the school to permit Pat to attend "in clothing and accessories that express her female gender identity" (*Doe v. Brockton Sch. Comm.*, 2000, p. 2). Jennifer Levi, the attorney who argued the case, summarized the decision as follows:

> We know that a large number of transgender students face serious hostility from teachers and administrators who lack a basic understanding about gender identity. This case confirms that a school may not exert its authority over a student simply to enforce stereotyped ideas of how boys and girls should look. Nor can a school's discomfort with the fact that a biologically male student has a female gender identity, justly enforce a dress code in a discriminatory way. (quoted in Gay and Lesbian Advocates and Defenders, 2000, p. 1)

This case is an important one for families and schools working to support the unique needs of transgender youth. Fortunately for Pat Doe, she had the support of her family, community advocates, and a knowledgeable therapist who could help advocate for her needs. In a related case in Toronto, Ontario, a student, "Jade," received appropriate support and guidance from her school when she transitioned from dressing and presenting as a boy to dressing and presenting as a girl in her school community. The case can provide a valuable case study for schools working with transgender students; for more details on how the Toronto District School Board worked with its staff to support Jade during her transition, see Callender, 2008. Unfortunately, many transgender youth do not have these avenues of support; therefore, it is incumbent upon schools to educate themselves on how to respect and value students' identities and offer them all the support and protection they need to safely attend and succeed in school.

CASE STUDY: CYBER-BULLYING

Case Seven: Casey Drews

Casey Drews was a student who reportedly was having social problems at her high school in Coeur d'Alene, Idaho. Some peers took a photo they found of her kissing a female friend, posted it on the Internet, and started spreading rumors at school that she was a lesbian. "Students called her names, avoided her, and would not undress for basketball games when she was in the room" (Brady & Conn, 2006, p. 9). Casey allegedly quit the basketball team and opted to be home-schooled as a result of these events.

Her parents took legal action against the school district for its "deliberate indifference" to the harassment under Title IX. This case was dismissed when the school demonstrated that Casey had not been deprived of educational services. Their lawyers produced affidavits proving that she did complete the basketball season and opted to be home-schooled in only one subject, science, by her own choosing (*Drews v. Joint School District*, 2006). Casey's experience indicates the extreme burden of proof that students and their families have when taking legal action against their school or school district. In this case, the school disproved the claim that Casey had been deprived of an educational service and thus did not have to address the other complaints related to her case.

The case law on cyber-bullying is quite limited to date, with few cases of students taking legal action against their schools. More commonly found cases include schools suing students for inappropriate online activities that insult or mock a school staff member or the school itself, such as *J.S. v. Bethlehem Area School District* (2002), *Layshock v. Hermitage School District* (2007), and *Emmett v. Kent School District,* (2000). As these are cases of schools suing students, they are beyond the purview of this book and won't be discussed here.

Although currently there are minimal legal precedents for cases of peer-to-peer cyber-bullying in schools, the existing case law on student expression and school safety is guiding the courts as they work to establish a legal framework for addressing online behavior that impacts the school environment. When taking action against a student for any kind of off-campus expression, schools must demonstrate that the content includes either a specific threat to a person's safety or information that substantially disrupts the learning environment of the school (*Tinker v. Des Moines Independent School District*, 1969). Scholars Kevin Brady and Kathleen Conn (2006) point out:

> Legal recognition of causes of action for cyberbullying against school boards may be longer in coming because of the difficulty in holding school boards and officials responsible for bullying and harassment that originate off campus, as is the case of cyberbullying that occurs when students post their bullying messages on the internet or in e-mails from home computers. (p. 9)

This is the challenge that legal cases involving cyber-bullying pose: Is it reasonable to hold schools responsible for students' behavior outside of school activities? Since cyber-bullying generally occurs on student-owned devices in out-of-school time, the school's role in monitoring and responding to such behaviors is limited. However, schools must recognize their responsibilities in teaching students responsible online behaviors and respond when incidents that start in cyberspace spill over and affect students' experiences in school.

In order to protect themselves from liability, individuals and schools need to be aware of their responsibilities in responding to incidents of bullying and harassment. The next section provides specific recommendations to help individuals and institutions reduce their legal liability in cases of peer harassment.

LESSONS LEARNED: RECOMMENDATIONS FOR REDUCING LIABILITY

School Staff

Teachers, nurses, school counselors, and administrators are all official representatives of the school and are each responsible for children's safety and well-being while at school. They can also be held individually responsible if they fail to effectively implement school and school district policies and procedures designed to protect students.

There are three important facts that school professionals need to be aware of when addressing incidents of bullying and harassment. First, if school personnel have witnessed incidents or a student has reported an incident, the school now has "actual knowledge" of the alleged harassment and must take action. If school personnel fail to report these incidents or do not follow school policy, they can be sued as individuals and may not be protected by the school district's liability insurance (*Nabozny v. Podlesny*, 1996). Second, individual punishments against certain perpetrators are necessary but not sufficient. As mentioned in the above case, *Doe v. Bellefonte Area School District*, teachers and administrators must work together to implement a series of graduated responses that include other members of the school staff and education for the student body. Finally, school personnel must respond consistently and fairly to all forms of reported harassment. As noted in the *Nabozny* case, if teachers and administrators severely punish one form of harassment, yet tend to ignore another, then they may be in violation of the Equal Protection Clause.

In order for school professionals to reduce their personal liability in cases of bullying and harassment, it is essential that they be aware of their school's policies and procedures for reporting and responding to bullying and harassment. Individuals must educate themselves about their roles and responsibilities in implementing school policies. Schools must also take affirmative steps to educate their staff about these policies.

Institutions

Schools and school districts are more likely than school staff to be targets for legal complaints from students, and their responsibilities at the institutional level are much more documented and clear. Fortunately, some detailed guidelines have emerged from the case law that schools and school boards can apply to reduce their liability. There are four main categories of recommended response for schools and school districts: staff training, student training, district policies, and staff conduct. They correspond directly with recommendations taken from the settlement agreement in the *Flores* case mentioned earlier. The following sections provide a detailed summary of the steps the school district was required to take in response to the court's decision and can act as a template for schools working to proactively address these issues as well.

Staff Training

The school district was required to implement a staff training program for administrators and "qualified staff." The court defined qualified staff as "certificated employees and all non-certificated staff or other employees who are responsible for monitoring student behavior. . . . [It] shall also include school custodians" (*Flores v. Morgan Hill*, 2004, p. 1). This mandatory training included an initial workshop and annual follow-up workshops of at least 3 hours—3.5 hours for administrators. The content of these sessions was to be devoted to the "recognition, investigation, and prevention of sexual orientation or gender identity harassment or discrimination" (*Flores v. Morgan Hill*, 2004, p. 2). Additionally, the administrators were required to discuss school safety, including the issue of sexual orientation and gender identity harassment or discrimination, at each bimonthly staff meeting and spend at least 1 hour each semester reviewing all policies and procedures regarding "the reporting, prevention of, and responses to incidents of sexual orientation or gender identity harassment or discrimination" (*Flores v. Morgan Hill*, 2004, p. 3) with teachers and support staff.

These were the minimum standards set out by the court settlement for staff training, and they underline the importance of regularly revisiting the issue and updating the staff's awareness of and attention to relevant policies and procedures. This is particularly important in schools where staff turnover is high.

Student Training

The settlement agreement also required some form of education for the student body. This student training program required that one 50-minute training session be offered to all students in grades 7 and 9 in a peer-to-peer format. These trainings could be integrated by the teachers into the already-existing curriculum with the support and guidance of an outside trainer. Students who transferred into the school district had to be provided with an orientation packet explaining the district's policies and procedures regarding sexual orientation and gender identity harassment or discrimination.

Working with the peer group is important, as it addresses the student body as a whole and ensures that students are aware of school policies and procedures as well as the school's stance on bullying and harassment. Schools must demonstrate that they have actively worked to educate the entire student body in cases where a single student is being targeted by multiple individuals. The importance of including workshops for the whole school on the topic of sexual orientation harassment was also listed as an essential response that was lacking in a similar Canadian case decided in favor of a student (*School District No. 44 v. Jubran*, 2005).

District Policies

In the *Flores* settlement, the school district was required to revise its policies to explicitly prohibit harassment and discrimination based on sexual orientation and gender. These policies had to be treated as a separate category of harassment and could not be included as a subset of sexual harassment. In addition to revising the policies, student handbooks and policy manuals also had to be rewritten to include the following information:

1. Detailed procedures for reporting and investigating allegations of harassment
2. A list of resources
3. A list of remedies and responses available for victims (*Flores v. Morgan Hill*, 2004, pp. 8-9)

The settlement also required that the school maintain a written record of complaints. These incident reports must include detailed information about the incident and the investigation, and they must be completed and filed within 15 days of a complaint.

Staff Conduct

The staff conduct portion of the settlement agreement included several elements: (1) compliance coordinators, (2) systems for reporting, and (3) enumeration of prohibited conduct. The first requirement of the staff conduct response involved appointing a "compliance coordinator" in each school to attend training and act as a resource person for the school community. The job of the compliance coordinator is to be familiar with and responsible for investigating, tracking, and advising students and staff in incidents of harassment or discrimination. The second requirement was to develop a protocol for reporting and responding to incidents of harassment and discrimination. The third requirement listed specific prohibited conduct of school district agents and employees, including failing to respond to complaints, engaging in harassing conduct, retaliating against complainants, or forcing a student out of the school community after making a harassment or discrimination complaint.

Although this settlement agreement was only required to be implemented until June 20, 2008, it is clear that the changes the school district made to comply will have lasting impacts beyond the end date of this agreement. Once policies have been revised, procedures have been implemented, and staff have been trained, the potential for lasting impacts of these institutional changes is strong. Schools can avoid high legal costs and stringent court-ordered changes by taking affirmative steps to include such policy and educational change voluntarily.

CONCLUSION

When educators proactively work to reduce the impacts of gendered harassment in their school communities, everyone benefits. Additionally, these actions will protect schools from legal and financial liability. Unfortunately, as was demonstrated in the above cases, the needs of targeted students often are ignored. The cases summarized in this chapter are meant to help educators better understand the legal mandates to create and maintain a school environment that allows every student to participate fully and does not discriminate. Chapter 6 provides schools with tangible steps to take in order to reduce the hostile climate created when harassing behaviors are prevalent.

CHAPTER 6

Transforming School Cultures

The problem with much of what has been said about bullying is the tendency of scholars, administrators, and teachers to look at it as isolated incidents perpetrated by problem students and thus ignore how cultural biases of sexism, homophobia, and transphobia impact how and who students bully. In order to develop effective strategies for intervention in schools, we must pay attention to the larger sociocultural forces that are at work. What we know and how we experience ourselves as individuals with multiple identities—such as gendered, religious, ethnic, and sexual—has a significant impact on how we see and interact with the world around us. This final chapter presents a summary of the main points of the research presented in this book and their implications for practice. It begins by synthesizing the main points from earlier chapters, and this is followed by a discussion of the main obstacles that prevent teachers from intervening effectively and consistently. The third section discusses practical suggestions aimed at transforming school cultures.

SUMMARY OF THE RESEARCH

To show how teachers perceive and respond to incidents of gendered harassment in secondary schools, I have developed a diagram to illustrate this theoretical model (Figure 6.1).

There are four tiers to this model that demonstrate the relationship between the main factors that influence how teachers perceive and respond to bullying and harassment in school: external influences, internal influences, perceptions of behaviors, and responses to behaviors. There are two categories of external influences (formal and informal) that get filtered through the teachers' internal influences (philosophies, identities, educational biographies, and life experiences). This interaction of external and internal influences shapes teachers' perceptions of and responses to student behaviors.

Figure 6.1. Factors Influencing Teachers' Noninterventions

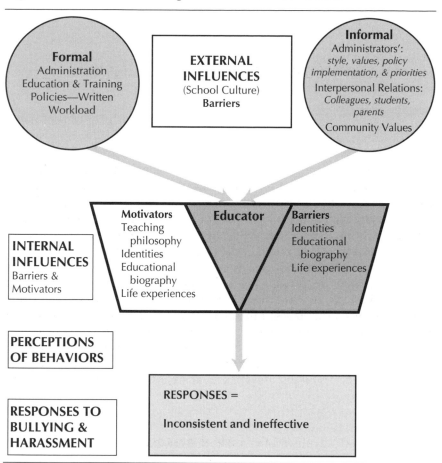

External Influences

As Chapter 3 explained, *formal* influences include administrative structures, school policies, teacher education, curriculum, and workload demands. These factors interact with informal influences to shape teachers' experiences of the school culture. *Informal* influences include the accepted norms and values in the school community and are absorbed from superiors (administration), peers (colleagues), students, and families/community members. The influence of administrators is significant in impacting how and when teachers chose to intervene in cases of bullying and harassment. It includes several aspects of school leadership, including administrators' style, personal values, professional priorities, and policy implementation. Other aspects of the informal school culture included colleagues' approaches to teaching and enforcing rules as well as the values endorsed by the student body and the surrounding community. The interaction between external and internal influences explains the wide variety of perceptions of and responses to gendered harassment by teachers.

Both external and internal influences present *barriers* to and *motivators* of teachers' interventions. These influences vary based on teachers' identities and experiences in their school cultures, but in most cases in this study, the barriers outweighed the motivators. The teachers reported that every aspect of these influences indicated that gendered harassment was accepted and the proactive responses against it would not be supported. This imbalance created a constant struggle for the teachers who were trying to reduce such behavior in their classrooms and schools but faced constant institutional resistance.

Institutional Resistance

The data collected in this study reflect Britzman's (2000) notions of the three forms of resistance to sexuality in schools: structural, pedagogical, and psychical. The findings show that the external factors create a majority of the barriers to effective intervention in cases of gendered harassment. Both formal and informal structures work to prevent effective education and response to bias around issues of sex, gender, and sexual orientation. Sources of *structural* resistance included administrators' style, policy implementation, and teacher workload demands. *Pedagogical* barriers included teacher education and training and provincial curriculum demands. *Psychical* barriers were found in administrators' and other teachers' personal values. Conversely, the teachers in this study had internal influences—such as their educational biographies, personal identities, and teaching philosophies—that motivated them to do their best to challenge gendered harassment in spite of the many formal and informal barriers in their schools.

Internal Influences

The teachers in this study all spoke of a deep awareness of and commitment to addressing incidents of bullying and harassment in school. If teachers do not have educational biographies or teaching philosophies that help them understand systemic oppressions such as sexism, transphobia, and homophobia, they may be less inclined to intervene. Additionally, if teachers do not believe in equality based on sex, sexual orientation, and gender identity or expression, their internal influences will act as additional barriers to confronting acts of gendered harassment when they occur. It is for this reason that teacher education programs must include a deeper understanding of diversity and equity issues related to sex, gender, and sexual orientation so that future educators can increase their awareness of and attention to these issues in schools. In addition to preparing teachers to offer instruction in their subject areas, these programs must encourage educators to think critically and reflect on their own identities and biases in order to better prepare them for working in increasingly diverse school communities.

Listening to teachers talk about their experiences with gendered harassment in schools, it became clear that it would not be possible for them to intervene effectively in incidences of gendered harassment until a shift in the entire school culture occurred. Indeed, they spoke about anti-gay jokes by their principals, sexual harassment perpetrated by their colleagues, and a general acceptance of sexist and homophobic language throughout the school.

RECOMMENDATIONS FOR CHANGE

Before embarking on the task of transforming a school's culture, it is important to acknowledge that every school is unique and that what may work in one school community may not be successful in another. Therefore, when trying to initiate any sort of school change, educators and community leaders must evaluate their own school communities before making decisions about what changes are necessary and possible and adjust these recommendations to their unique situation. This approach should improve the chances of successful and long-term change.

The theoretical model presented above can be a useful tool for analyzing and transforming school cultures. The school culture is a product of the institutional structures (formal) and societal norms and values (informal) that work together to privilege certain behaviors and experiences over others. These are shaped by directives and decisions made at the school district and state level, but the individuals who spend every day together in the school buildings are also implicated in creating and sustaining these environments. As other bullying and harassment researchers have pointed out (Cartwright, 1995; Duncan, 2004; Eder, 1997; Olweus, 1993), in order for interventions to be effective, a shift in the culture of the school must occur.

I begin by making recommendations for administrators, as it has been repeatedly asserted that school leadership is a key factor in creating and sustaining the culture of the school. Next I offer strategies for teachers, which includes building alliances among colleagues. Third, I make suggestions for students and offer recommendations that recognize the powerful influence of youth cultures and student action in shaping the school environment. Finally, I address the role of families and community members in these efforts.

Administration

Leadership

The teachers in this study spoke extensively about their principals and vice principals and how the identities and leadership styles of these administrators impacted how individual teachers would respond to different situations. Many teachers perceived their principals and vice principals as being somewhat sexist and homophobic. These perceptions were offered as reasons for not being able to more effectively reduce the amount of gendered harassment occurring in their classrooms and the school community. The power that administrators have to shape and influence their school environments has been widely documented (Carr, 1997; Dinham, Cairney, Craigie, & Wilson, 1995; Fullan, 2000; Riehl, 2000). Administrators' actions are grounded in subjective interpretations that arise from their own personal biographies, which are situated within collective histories of their cultural groups (Dillard cited in Riehl, 2000). This means that educational leadership programs need to work proactively to develop a more critical understanding of and approach to understanding bias in their schools and communities. School boards also need to place a higher priority on diversifying the demographics of those they hire as school leaders. As Carolyn Riehl (2000) points out, "If practice is connected to identity, then it matters who administrators are" (p. 70).

Principals and vice principals must respond consistently to acts of gendered harassment and must role-model this position for their staff. They need to investigate complaints thoroughly and document the steps they have taken to remedy situations reported to them. They must also work to educate themselves about sex, gender, and sexual orientation and address these issues explicitly in all conversations about equity, safety, and success in school. One formal tool that school leaders have to reshape school cultures is revising and actively implementing school policies.

Policy

In order to be effective, school policies must be publicly displayed and easy to understand. Essential elements of successful policies include the following:

1. Community consultation
2. Clear language
3. An implementation plan
4. Procedural guidelines
5. An evaluation phase

Community consultation is an important step in developing a broad base of support for policy changes and allowing members to voice concerns early in the process. By including various stakeholders when revising policy, leaders can anticipate opposition and find ways to meet the objectives of a more inclusive school environment. *Clear language* allows all members of the community to understand who will be affected by the policy. Including a complete list of protected groups as well as guidelines regarding prohibited language and behavior are ways to make existing policies more effective. Though some might argue that adding a "laundry list" of marginalized groups could weaken or limit a policy, history has shown that full equality and protection are not granted to oppressed groups until a list of protected classes is established. When updating the language in harassment policies, it is also important to include an action plan for dealing with incidents of cyber-bullying.

An *implementation plan* is also crucial for meaningful success (Sharp & Smith, 1991). If members of the school community are unaware that a policy change has happened or don't know how it affects their roles, then changes will not come about. Plans are most effective that include three main items:

1. A list of the roles and responsibilities of students, families, and staff
2. An education and awareness campaign to inform all members of the school community of the new policy
3. Financial and administrative support for staff development in relation to the new policy

If school staff don't feel that they have the tools or knowledge to effectively implement a new policy, then they are unlikely to support it in meaningful ways. One way to guide school staff in the implementation of a new policy is to provide them with suggested procedures to follow when responding to incidents of gendered harassment. Response protocols will vary depending on the population and the setting of the school, but they are useful guidelines for educators to refer to when a shift in school climate is under way. As Ian Macgillivray points out, "the way in which the policy is implemented has direct bearing on how the new policy is received and perceived by the teachers" (2004, p. 63).

Finally, an *evaluation phase* is an essential step in determining where
the policy has been implemented successfully and where more determined
efforts are needed. Policies should be evaluated within 2 or 3 years to ensure
that they are being followed consistently throughout the school. This is an
area where many efforts fall short, but it holds great potential for lasting
success in reshaping school cultures.

Teachers

Teachers must work within the guidelines of their school's policies to address
incidents of bullying and harassment, and they can also play a key role in
initiating policy and climate changes in their school community. Teachers
can take these steps in three main ways:

1. Building alliances with colleagues to create a unified front in
    responding to bullying and harassment
2. Pursuing opportunities to learn more about how to address gender,
    bullying, and harassment effectively
3. Creating an organized response protocol for their classroom that
    supports school policy and matches your teaching style

In order to *build alliances*, teachers can start by working informally with a
small group of colleagues to discuss bullying and harassment in their school.
By exchanging ideas and expertise, teachers can develop a supportive group
of colleagues who can start implementing a more consistent response to bullying and harassment in all areas of the school. Teachers can also attempt to
persuade department heads or vice principals to allocate staff meeting time
to discuss school policy and intervention protocols.

Teachers can also *pursue opportunities* for their own ongoing professional development. Teachers must recognize their own blind spots and take
proactive steps to improve their own understanding of issues that they find
challenging. They can read books and articles, attend community events,
and seek out sessions at teachers' conferences on these topics. Although
much of this effort is a teacher's own responsibility, it can only be effective
and sustainable with the support of the school. Schools can support this
work by paying conference fees, offering pedagogical development days to
teachers to attend workshops of the teachers' choosing, and creating a culture that values ongoing development in its staff.

Related to issues of professional development is workload. The emphasis on "covering material" and preparing for high-stakes exams forces
teachers to attempt to teach large amounts of curricular content and ignore student misbehavior and other issues of community and citizenship.

One way to address this problem is to create a *response protocol* to be implemented in the classroom. Whether it is creating a classroom contract, tracking student behaviors in a lesson book, establishing an escalating punishment plan, or structuring a reporting procedure, having a system in place will make it much easier to address these incidents when they occur. For example, I would have students in my classes write a note explaining the incident to give to me at the end of class. I could then pass this on to a parent, administrator, or counselor with my explanation of the events. This reduced the amount of instructional time lost and prompted students to take responsibility for their actions as well as giving them the opportunity to explain their version of the event.

Students

Students are often overlooked when policy changes are made. They are viewed as passive participants rather than active creators of the school culture. Students comprise the largest percentage of a school community and are the trend-setters for what is valued in school. Without the support of student leaders, there will continue to be student-only spaces where incidents of harassment take place, such as locker areas, washrooms, playgrounds, and athletic fields. Schools that successfully engage student leaders—such as athletic team captains, student council members, peer mediators, and others—can have a much broader and deeper impact on the lives of all students. Ways that this can be done include the following:

1. Implementing a more student-centered approach to teaching and coaching
2. Integrating a critical and queer pedagogy across the curriculum (Meyer, 2007, 2008a)
3. Introducing extracurricular projects such as summer leadership retreats, after-school discussion groups on diversity issues, or weekend workshops that educate students about bullying and harassment

Workshops and discussion groups can provide a forum about school culture and solicit students' help and support in challenging gendered harassment and other forms of bias in the school. In addition to engaging prominent students in the school population, all students should be informed of the school's policies on harassment and discrimination by posting a code of conduct in each classroom, having students sign a behavior contract, and/ or having homeroom and team discussions about the policy, what it means, and how it might affect them.

Families and Community Members

Finally, the input and influence of families and community members are important. The parents' association and other community groups should be encouraged to become actively involved in developing the school policy and educational strategies regarding bullying and harassment. By developing these partnerships early on, schools can anticipate any resistance or potential backlash and work through these issues before they grow into negative publicity for the school. Most families are deeply invested in the education and development of their children and therefore should be included in such initiatives. However, sometimes the values taught at home might conflict with the goals and mission of the school. This is a delicate situation, but an important one to address. Teachers and administrators must feel supported in explicitly teaching the stated values of the school even if they may go against the religious and cultural values of some students' families. Public schools have a responsibility to prepare students for active citizenship in a democracy. As such, it is important for them to teach the kinds of behavior, language, and interactions that are expected in public settings. By informing parents of the expectations of the school community and consistently supporting these values in newsletters, school events, and other interactions with family members, students will learn which behaviors are appropriate in certain settings and which are not.

Although there may be resistance from some families to creating a school that values gender and sexual diversity, by building strong ties with parent groups and other community and religious organizations, schools can create a lasting network that will potentially expand their efforts to reduce such bias in the community at large.

By working with all four groups of stakeholders in a school community, we drastically improve our chances of lasting and meaningful change in the culture of the school. Each of these four groups actively participates in creating and supporting the formal and informal cultures of the school and must be included in any approach to reduce gendered harassment and related forms of bias in schools.

GETTING STARTED: A CHECKLIST

It can often feel overwhelming to imagine how to tackle these issues in a way that will have a lasting impact. In order to not be paralyzed by the large tasks that lie ahead, it can be helpful to start with small steps. This means beginning with lower-risk activities and finding allies within a school community before taking on some of the larger, more systemic changes. I have adapted a format created by Arthur Lipkin and incorporated information from other sources to provide stepping-stones to take clear action toward reducing gendered harassment in schools and communities (Goldstein, 2001; Lipkin, 1999; Macgillivray, 2007; Perrotti & Westheimer, 2001).

1. *Educate yourself about sex, gender, and sexual orientation and the related bias categories of sexism, heterosexism, transphobia, and homophobia.*
   A. Low Risk
      ▶ Learn about gay, lebian, bisexual, and transgender(GLBT) history, culture, leaders, and current concerns by reading books and periodicals and viewing films. See Appendix A for some ideas.
      ▶ Study women's history and examine how expectations based on gender impact people's opportunities in school and careers.
      ▶ Read *My Gender Workbook* (Bornstein, 1998), a fun and interactive resource that helps show how gender shapes everyday interactions and decisions.
      ▶ Watch *Tough Guise* (Katz, 2002), an accessible educational film on masculinity and the media.
   B. Some Risk
      ▶ Attend a public lecture or film series on GLBT or gender issues.
      ▶ Attend a meeting of a local support or advocacy group for GLBT allies (P-FLAG, COLAGE, GLSEN).
   C. Greater Risk
      ▶ Invite a friend or colleague to join you at a film or lecture that addresses sexism, homophobia, or transphobia.
      ▶ Engage friends, family, and colleagues in conversations about issues in your community related to gender, bullying, and harassment.

2. *Create a safer and more equitable classroom.*
   A. Low Risk
      ▶ Challenge your own assumptions that everyone is heterosexual unless they tell you otherwise.
      ▶ Use inclusive language that allows for diverse family structures (*parent* or *guardian*, rather than *mother* and *father*; *partner* or *spouse* rather than *husband* or *wife*).

▶ Avoid gender-specific language and assumptions in class activities (such as asking girls to help clean and boys to help move heavy things; saying "boys don't cry" or "don't act like a girl").

B. Some Risk

▶ "Stop and educate" anytime you hear negative or harassing language in your classroom:

- Educate privately to be sure the students involved understand why their language and behaviors were inappropriate. OR
- Educate publicly to model taking a stand and set a precedent in front of other students.

▶ Put up posters and brochures in your classroom that celebrate accomplishments by diverse people: women, GLBT people, people of color, and so on.

▶ If you are heterosexual, don't state it. Allow yourself to be an ally while allowing others to be uncertain about your sexual orientation.

▶ Explore social networking Web sites and popular video games so you are aware of current trends and slang in youth culture.

C. Greater Risk

▶ Actively include issues relating to sexual orientation and gender identity in your classes.

▶ Invite GLBT speakers to address your class.

▶ If you are GLBT, come out to your employer, and if you get his or her support, come out to your students and school.

3. *Create a safer and more equitable school.*

A. Low Risk

▶ Model celebration of and respect for diversity.

▶ Pass this book on to a colleague to read.

B. Some Risk

▶ "Stop and educate" anytime you hear negative or harassing language in public areas (hall, cafeteria, bathrooms, locker rooms, etc.)

▶ Help students establish a Gay–Straight Alliance or other diversity group in your school.

▶ Request and/or help organize staff training on issues related to gendered harassment and cyber-bullying.

▶ Build a network of colleagues interested in starting a safety and equity task force at your school.

- ▶ Revise and update school policies to address gendered harassment and cyber-bullying.
- ▶ Ask your school librarian to order books and resources that address these issues—some targeted toward students and some toward staff.

C. Greater Risk

- ▶ Work with students to organize a "Day of Silence" (www.dayofsilence.org).
- ▶ Work with colleagues to organize a "No Name Calling Week" (www.nonamecallingweek.org)
- ▶ Invite parents, religious leaders, and community members to work on a safety and equity task force in your school and community.
- ▶ Ask your school librarian to create a display of books and resources on sex, gender, and sexual orientation.
- ▶ Encourage colleagues to integrate issues related to sex, gender, and sexual orientation diversity in their curricula.
- ▶ Invite speakers and performance groups that address multiple issues of diversity, including sex, gender, and sexual orientation.

CONCLUSION

Gender is a major factor in most incidents of bullying and harassment because it is a powerful force in shaping human behavior. Asking people to think differently about how we understand gender and how it relates to bullying, harassment, sexuality, and schooling is often controversial and challenging. Questioning traditional notions of masculinity and femininity is like tearing down the walls of the house we grew up in. These are the values that we grew up with, the rules that we spent our childhood learning to follow and decode, and the history that all of our shared stories are embedded in. They are familiar. It is what we know. They are so familiar that they have become invisible and are not talked about or reexamined. Although that childhood home can be familiar and comfortable for some, it can be restricting and suffocating for many. Unfortunately, familiar walls of gender that define so many of our behaviors and relationships don't allow for the range of identities and experiences that exist in our world. These boundaries have been carefully taught and monitored, but in order to make room for everyone, they need to be looked at, questioned, and reconstructed.

There is much work to be done. States and school districts need to write and/or revise laws and policies to explicitly include protections based on gender identity/expression and sexual orientation. Administrators need to initiate a process of school change that starts with updating school-level policies and manuals and educating themselves about these issues. Sexual harassment, sexual orientation harassment, and harassment for gender nonconformity need to be named separately from bullying in all policies and documents in order to effectively end them. If you can't even name the target, how can you expect to reach it? By modeling a dedication to these issues, administrators can empower the school staff to be more proactive in addressing gendered harassment.

Teachers and other school staff need to work together to consistently respond to acts of gendered harassment that they witness. They need to understand the long-term impacts of these negative behaviors and their responsibilities in ending them. Students and families must also be actively engaged in this process to ensure lasting and meaningful change.

This book is just one of many available resources out there to help parents, teachers, administrators, and teacher educators to take action to reduce gendered harassment in schools. It is not easy work, and there are many obstacles along the way. It is my hope that by providing some resources and guidelines this will empower youth and educators to take a stand against sexism, homophobia, transphobia, and heteronormativity in their schools and to value and include students and families of all sexual orientations and gender expressions.

APPENDIX A

Resources

The key to the cost of available resources for use in classrooms with students and professional development workshops is as follows:

$ = $50 or less
$$ = $50–$150
$$$ = $150–500
$$$$ = $500+

SCHOOLWIDE INTERVENTIONS

Ally Week (Free)

www.glsen.org/allyweek

This event, organized by the Gay, Lesbian, and Straight Education Network, is held every October to end anti-GLBT bullying and harassment in K-12 schools by building ties with "allies." Allies are identified as people who advocate for the equality of a marginalized group but do not identify as a member of that group. In the case of this event, most allies identify as heterosexual or *cisgendered*. The goal of this event is to get students to sign an ally pledge to intervene in incidents of anti-GLBT bullying and harassment.

Challenge Day ($$$$)

www.challengeday.org

This nonprofit community-building initiative can be a valuable way to jump-start anti-bullying and anti-harassment work in a school. It can be somewhat costly for a school community since the organization's travel costs must be paid for if their trip is more than 1 hour from Concord, California. The school community must also guarantee a minimum of 3 (up to a maximum of 4) consecutive Challenge Program days at 1 school or 2 within 1 hour's driving distance from each other. However, it has proven to be a powerful and healing experience that has positive impacts on the culture of schools as well as on the students who participate. Some of the activities explicitly address issues of systemic oppression, including gender and sexual orientation. The goal of this event is "to build connection and empathy, and to fulfill our vision that every child lives in a world where they feel safe, loved, and celebrated."

Day of Silence (Free)
www.dayofsilence.org
This somewhat controversial event began in 1996 at the University of Virginia when a group of students chose to remain silent for one day to call attention to the anti-GLBT name-calling and harassment at their school. In 2007, over 5,000 middle and high schools registered to participate. There has been backlash in some communities against this event, but students and teachers who have participated indicate that it is a nonconfrontational yet empowering way to highlight these issues in a school community. This Web site provides guidance and free resources to help student groups organize this event in their school community.

The International Day Against Homophobia (Free)
http://www.homophobiaday.org/
This annual educational campaign was started in 2003 in Quebec to increase public awareness about homophobia. This Web site provides informational posters and publications for schools and other organizations to participate in the activities on May 17 and year-round.

Mix It Up at Lunch (Free)
http://www.tolerance.org/teens/lunch.jsp
This annual event encourages students to break out of their cliques and cross divisions in their school's social culture at lunchtime. Sponsored by the Southern Poverty Law Center's Teaching Tolerance program.

No Name Calling Week (Free/$$)
www.nonamecallingweek.org
Inspired by James Howe's novel *The Misfits*, this event has grown into a nationwide phenomenon since it was first organized in March 2004. There are free downloadable resources on the Web site as well as a kit that can be purchased online. This is targeted toward students in grades 5–8 and explicitly addresses biased forms of name-calling and harassment that occur between students, including those affecting homophobia. Many schoolwide organizing ideas as well as classroom activities are available.

Olweus Bullying Prevention Program (Guide $$; Training $$$$)
http://www.clemson.edu/olweus/
The schoolwide intervention kit provides all the information necessary to conduct a schoolwide survey and interventions for a school community. This program offers school-level, classroom-level, and individual-level components for training and community involvement. The program highly recommends using its trainers when implementing program. Although this is one of the most widely studied bullying intervention programs, with a documented record of reducing incidents of overt bullying, its focus on behavioral interventions and lack of attention to issues of sex, gender, sexual orientation, and other forms of bias indicate that it may not be as effective in reducing forms of gendered harassment.

Ugly Ducklings **(Free to Schools in Maine/$$)**
www.uglyducklings.org
This film and educational kit come designed to promote dialogue around issues connected to teen suicide and homophobia. The film follows a group of young women at a summer retreat and allows the participants to share their emotional experiences as they learn and talk about these issues.

STAFF DEVELOPMENT

Challenging Silence, Challenging Censorship **($)**
http://www.ctf-fce.ca/e/publications/ctf_publications.asp
This is a valuable guide for librarians and other educators interested in providing resources and support for GLBT youth, families, and their allies. It provides an annotated bibliography of books and materials for students of all ages.

GLSEN Lunchbox **($$)**
www.glsenstore.org
This training toolkit provides many interactive activities, videos, and fact sheets on GLBT issues in schools. It is valuable for consultants, resource centers, and organizations that provide educators with in-service training and support on issues related to sex, gender, and sexual orientation. GLSEN also provides training institutes on using the toolkit effectively and developing facilitators' skills.

It Takes a Team **(Free/$)**
www.ittakesateam.org
This kit specifically addresses how gender and sexual orientation stereotypes can harm athletes, coaches, and the team environment. The kit includes a

video, action guides, posters, stickers, and additional resources that can be helpful for coaches and athletes at the secondary and university level.

It's Elementary: Talking About Gay Issues in Schools ($$)
http://www.groundspark.org/films/elementary/
This now-classic video and its accompanying discussion guide are an excellent teaching resource for age-appropriate ways to talk about gay and lesbian issues with elementary-age students. A particular strength of this video is that it has footage from actual classroom activities and discussions. It also does an excellent job including the experiences of students from different regions of the United States and of diverse ethnic and cultural backgrounds. A second film, *It's STILL Elementary,* that follows up with students from the original film is now available as well.

Just Call Me Kade ($$)
http://cart.frameline.org/ProductDetails.asp?ProductCode=T526
This award-winning documentary video traces the transition of an adolescent FTM (female to male) transgendered person. It provides a valuable first-person narrative for those who are new to learning about transgender issues.

Lessons Learned ($)
http://www.ctf-fce.ca/e/publications/ctf_publications.asp
This short publication from the Canadian Teachers' Federation provides a brief introduction to terminology and studies as well as a collection of stories and experiences from educators working in anti-homophobia education. It is a useful aid in understanding the cultural and political contexts for addressing GLBT issues in Canadian schools.

Seeking Educational Equity and Diversity (SEED) ($$$$)
http://www.wcwonline.org/?option=com_content&task=view&id=893&Itemid=54
For more than 20 years the National SEED Project on Inclusive Curriculum, a staff development equity project for educators, has been providing teacher-led faculty development seminars in public and private schools throughout the United States and in English-speaking international schools. A week-long SEED summer New Leaders' Workshop prepares teachers to hold year-long reading groups with other teachers to discuss making school climates and curricula more gender-fair and multiculturally equitable.

Teaching Respect for All ($)
www.glsenstore.org

This training video captures a compelling talk given to an audience of teachers, administrators, and counselors by Kevin Jennings, GLSEN executive director, author, and former high school teacher. He is a dynamic speaker, and this video captures the key points for educators to understand when addressing homophobia and GLBT issues in schools.

K-12 CLASSROOM

Bullyproof: A Teacher's Guide on Teasing and Bullying ($)
http://www.wcwonline.org/
This book, a classic classroom resource, is a practical guide for teachers wanting to address issues of gender, bullying, and harassment with students in grades 4–6. With lesson plans, handouts, and activity guides, this affordable resource can help teachers address these issues in age-appropriate ways with younger kids. There is a specific focus on sexual harassment and discussions of gender roles, but no inclusion of issues relating to sexual orientation or homophobia.

Dealing with Differences ($)
www.glsenstore.org
This video and teacher guide, available from GLSEN, show teachers how to introduce conversations about respect and anti-GLBT harassment into the secondary classroom (grades 7–12).

Flirting or Hurting? ($)
http://www.wcwonline.org/
This book is a practical guide for teachers wanting to address the topic of sexual harassment with students in grades 7–12. With lesson plans, handouts, and activity guides, this affordable resource can help teachers address issues related to sexual harassment in ways linked specifically to their content areas. There is a specific focus on sexual harassment and discussions of gender roles, but no inclusion of issues relating to sexual orientation or homophobia.

Gender Doesn't Limit You! (Free)
http://www.tolerance.org/teach/activities/activity.jsp?ar=841&ttnewsletter=ttnewsgen-091307
This series of six lesson plans combines information on reducing gender stereotypes in early grades (K–4) with bullying intervention strategies. Researchers working on this project found that this curriculum successfully increased students' willingness to take a stand to counteract bullying.

GLSEN (Free/$)

http://www.glsen.org/cgi-bin/iowa/all/library/curriculum.html
This nonprofit organization has a Web site that is full of free downloadable lesson plans (K–12) and reading lists (sorted by age) to assist teachers interested in integrating information about sex, gender, and sexual orientation as well as related forms of diversity education into their classes.

Let's Get Real! ($$)

http://www.groundspark.org/films/letsgetreal/index.html
This video and curriculum guide address multiple forms of bias and harassment that occur in schools. They provide firsthand narratives from students who have been targeted as well as from students who have taken a stand on behalf of others. The wide variety of issues covered in the video provide a valuable starting point for talking about bias and harassment with students in grades 6–12.

Media Awareness Network (Free)

www.media-awareness.ca
This bilingual site (French and English) provides a rich variety of lesson plans and resources on gender and stereotypes using media texts. Teachers can search by grade level (K–12) or topic for classroom activities and resources.

Tough Guise ($$)

http://www.mediaed.org/
This educational video is geared toward high school students to help them examine the relationships between popular culture images and the construction of masculinity. This entertaining and well-researched video provides an engaging approach to understanding how gender and violence are related and the pressure on boys to put on a "tough guise." The Media Education Foundation has a wealth of other resources on gender, sexual orientation, and the media on its Web site.

ADDITIONAL READING

Bochenek, M., & Brown, A. W. (2001). *Hatred in the hallways: Violence and discrimination against lesbian, gay, bisexual, and transgender students in U.S. schools*: New York: Human Rights Watch.

    This important study summarizes the often painful and difficult experiences of GLBT students in schools around the United States and provides a concise summary of legal protections that exist for GLBT students in U.S. schools.

Brown, L. M. (2003). *Girlfighting: Betrayal and rejection among girls.* New York: New York University Press.

> *This book by respected gender scholar Lyn Mikel Brown synthesizes the voices of over 400 interviews with girls in the United States and provides an insightful analysis of the gender issues involved in relationships among girls.*

Duncan, N. (1999). *Sexual bullying: Gender conflict and pupil culture in secondary schools.* London: Routledge.

> *This book summarizes the findings of a ethnographic study of a secondary school in England and provides detailed analyses of the role of gender, sex, and sexual orientation in influencing peer relations in the school community.*

Mac an Ghaill, M. (1995). *The making of men: Masculinities, sexualities, and schooling.* Philadelphia: Open University Press.

> *This was one of the first books to explore the connections among masculinity, homophobia, bullying, and social relations in school. It is a very rich and nuanced analysis of varying forms of masculinity in school.*

Macgillivray, I. K. (2007). *Gay–straight alliances: A handbook for students, educators, and parents.* New York: Harrington Park Press.

> *This concise and easy-to-read guide provides practical advice and detailed resources for students, teachers, administrators, and parents engaged in creating or working with Gay–Straight Alliances.*

Olweus, D. (1993). *Bullying at school: What we know and what we can do.* Oxford: Blackwell.

> *This is the seminal book on bullying published by the originator of bullying research. It provides a helpful foundation for understanding how most schools frame their responses to general bullying but does not include an understanding of bullying as gendered behavior.*

Pascoe, C.J. (2007) *Dude you're a fag: Masculinity and sexuality in high school.* Berkeley: University of California Press.

> *This book provides an incisive view of how masculinity is regulated and negotiated based on a recent study in one California high school.*

Perrotti, J., & Westheimer, K. (2001). *When the drama club is not enough: Lessons from the Safe Schools Program for Gay and Lesbian Students.* Boston: Beacon Press.

> *This book is a practical and informative guide based on the work and experiences of educators working in Massachusetts with the first statewide program aimed at supporting GLBT youth in schools.*

Shariff, S. (2008). *Cyberbullying: Issues and solutions for the school, the classroom and the home.* New York: Routledge.

> *This is the most comprehensive resource currently available on the issue of cyber-bullying. It provides valuable policy guidance for school lawyers and administrators as well as an entire chapter dedicated to issues of gender in cyberspace.*

Glossary

bisexual. A person who is attracted to some members of both sexes to varying degrees. The prefix *bi* indicates the belief that there are only two sexes. See also: *omnisexual, pansexual*

bullying. According to Oweus (1993), "A student is being bullied or victimized when he or she is exposed, repeatedly and over time, to negative actions on the part of one or more other students . . . it is a negative action when someone intentionally inflicts, or attempts to inflict, injury or discomfort on another. . . . Negative actions can be carried out by words (verbally), for instance, by threatening, taunting, teasing, and calling names. It is a negative action when somebody hits, pushes, kicks, pinches or restrains another—by physical contact. It is also possible to carry out negative actions without the use of words or physical contact, such as by making faces or dirty gestures, intentionally excluding someone from a group, or refusing to comply with another person's wishes" (p. 9).

cisgender. This term is borrowed from chemistry to describe individuals whose gender identity and expression aligns with social expectations for their sex assigned at birth. It is used in contrast with the term "transgender."

compulsory heterosexuality. The theory advanced by poet and lesbian feminist Adrienne Rich (1978/1993) that women are coerced by social structures to engage in heterosexual relationships with men. She argues that heterosexuality is a political institution, not just a naturally occurring phenomenon, and is a central feature of patriarchy.

discourse. Linguistic practices that shape social relations and cultural beliefs. Based in the work of French philosopher Michel Foucault, it is considered to be the institutionalized way of thinking as established by how and what words are used in certain contexts (see also Jaworski & Coupland, 1999).

euroheteropatriarchy. A term advanced by Francisco Valdez (2002) that provides a shorthand term for "the interlocking operation of dominant forms racism, ethnocentrism, androcentrism, and heterocentrism—all of which operate in tandem in the United States and beyond it to produce identity hierarchies that subordinate people of color, women, and sexual minorities in different yet similar and familiar ways" (p. 404).

gay. The preferred term for a person who engages in same-sex relationships and identifies as a member of this community. It is preferred to the term *homosexual*, which has scientific meanings that apply specifically to same-sex behaviors and does not consider a person's identities and relationships. *Gay* can refer to both men and women, although many women prefer the term *lesbian*.

gender. A term used to describe those characteristics of women and men that are socially constructed, in contrast to those that are legally and biologically determined—that is, sex. People are assigned a sex at birth but learn to act like girls and boys who grow into women and men. They are taught what the appropriate behaviors, attitudes, roles, and activities are for them and how they should relate to other people. These learned attributes are what make up gender identity and expression as well as determine gender roles.

gender expression. How one chooses to dress, walk, talk, and accessorize to express one's gender identity. Related terms include *gender role performance* and *gender presentation*.

gender identity. Refers to an individual's innate sense of self as a man, woman, transgender, genderqueer, or other identification. This is often shaped by one's sex assigned at birth and the gender in which a person is raised. It may change over time and may not fit into the traditional dichotomous gender categories of man/woman.

gender nonconformity. When a person's gender expression varies from that which is traditionally expected for a person of that sex; for example, when a male shows an interest in dance or fashion, or when a female enjoys rough and aggressive sports and activities.

gendered harassment. Any unwanted behavior that polices and reinforces the traditional notions of heterosexual masculinity and heterosexual femininity and includes (hetero)sexual harassment, homophobic harassment, and harassment for gender nonconformity (Meyer, 2006).

GLBT. Abbreviation for gay, lesbian, bisexual, and transgender people.

harassment. Biased behaviors that have a negative impact on the target or the environment (Land, 2003). They may be intentional or unintentional.

harassment for gender nonconformity. Any unwanted behavior that targets a person's perceived masculinity or femininity. Also referred to as transphobic harassment.

hegemonic masculinity. From a theory advanced by Robert Connell (1995) it is the form of masculinity that occupies a dominant and privileged position in a given pattern of gender relations. In Western cultures, this can be often defined by claims to authority (often through aggression, physical strength, dominance, institutional power) and heterosexuality but is subject to change if social relations shift.

heteronormativity. A term coined by Michael Warner (1991) to describe a system of behaviors and social expectations that are built around the belief that everyone is or should be heterosexual and that all relationships and families follow this model. See also *compulsory heterosexuality*; *heterosexism*; and *heterosexual matrix*.

heterosexism. A bias toward heterosexuality that denigrates and devalues GLB people. Also, the presumption that heterosexuality is superior to homosexuality or prejudice, bias, or discrimination based on these things.

(hetero)sexual harassment. Any unwanted behavior that has a sexual or gender component and is enacted within the matrix of heterosexual relations. It includes two main types of harassment: quid pro quo and hostile environment. Quid pro quo harassment is an explicit offer of an exchange, such as, "I will give you a better grade if you do a sexual favor for me." Hostile environment harassment is more common in schools and includes any behavior that acts to create a hostile environment, such as graffiti, jokes, comments, gestures, looks, and unwanted touching.

heterosexual matrix. A concept advanced by gender theorist Judith Butler (1990) that builds on Adrienne Rich's notion of compulsory heterosexuality. Butler states that all gender relations are built within the boundaries of the "oppositionally and hierarchically defined . . . compulsory practice of heterosexuality" (p. 194).

homophobia. Fear or hatred of those assumed to be GLBT and anything connected to their culture. When a person fears homosexuality, either in other people or within the self, homophobia can involve attitudes or behavior that range from mild discomfort to verbally abusive or physically violent acts.

homophobic harassment. See *sexual orientation harassment*.

lesbian. The preferred term for a woman who engages in same-sex relationships and identifies as a member of this community. It is preferred to the term homosexual, which has scientific meanings that apply specifically to same-sex behaviors and does not consider a person's identities and relationships.

omnisexual. A person who is attracted to some members of any sex to varying degrees. The prefix *omni* comes from the Latin for "all" and indicates the belief that there are many sexes.

pansexual. A person who is attracted to some members of all sexes to varying degrees. The prefix "pan," from the Greek for "all," indicates the belief that there are many sexes.

patriarchy. The basic definition of a patriarchy is a society that is governed and controlled by men. Feminist theorists have used this term to explain the current gender system that gives males access to power and social privileges and in turn marginalizes and oppresses people of all other genders. See also *heterosexism*; *sexism*.

sex. A medico-legal category that is assigned at birth based on certain biological characteristics that vary by region. Such characteristics may include a child's chromosomes, gonadal tissue, hormone levels, and external genitalia. Sexual dimorphism is often thought to be a scientific reality, whereas individuals who are intersex point to a multiplicity of sexes in the human population. This is different from gender, which is sociocultural, as noted above.

sexism. The belief or attitude that women are inferior to men, also related to misogyny. This results in oppression and discrimination against women in patriarchal societies.

sexual harassment. See *(hetero)sexual harassment*

sexual orientation. This term describes the genders and sexes to which a person is emotionally, physically, romantically, and erotically attracted—such as homosexual, bisexual, omnisexual, heterosexual, and asexual—and is informed by innate sexual attraction. In all instances, this term should be used instead of *sexual preference* or other misleading terminology. Trans and gender-variant people may identify with any sexual orientation, and their sexual orientation may or may not change before, during, or after transition.

sexual orientation harassment. Any unwanted behavior that insults or harms gays, lesbians, and bisexuals, or uses anti-GLB insults to insult or harm another person. May be targeted at GLB people or non-GLB people.

social construct. This concept emerged from sociology and psychology to describe concepts and terms that exist because a society or culture has collectively decided to agree that it exists. Some examples include money, citizenship, race, and gender.

transgender. An umbrella term, like *trans*, for individuals who blur the lines of traditional gender expression, usually including transsexual and sometimes also including cross-dressers. These individuals may or may not choose to change physical characteristics of their bodies or legally change their sex.

transphobia. The irrational fear and hatred of all individuals who transgress, violate, or blur the dominant gender categories in a given society. Transphobic attitudes can lead to discrimination, violence, and oppression against the gay, lesbian, bisexual, trans, and intersex communities as well as gender-nonconforming individuals.

transphobic harassment. See *harassment for gender nonconformity*

verbal harassment. Persistent and repeated negative behaviors that are unwanted and verbal in nature, such as name-calling, insults, sexual jokes, and graffiti. As with other forms of harassment, it may be intentional or unintentional.

References

ACLU. (2004). Settlement fact sheet: *Flores v. Morgan Hill Unified School District*. Retrieved March 28, 2006, from www.aclu.org

Adair, V., Dixon, R. S., Moore, D. W., & Sutherland, C. M. (2000). Ask your mother not to make yummy sandwiches: Bullying in New Zealand secondary schools. *New Zealand Journal of Educational Studies, 35*(2), 207–221.

Agatston, P. W., Kowalski, R., & Limber, S. (2007). Students' perspectives on cyber bullying. *Journal of Adolescent Health, 41*(6, Suppl), S59–S60.

Bagley, C., Bolitho, F., & Bertrand, L. (1997). Sexual assault in school, mental health and suicidal behaviors in adolescent women in Canada. *Adolescence, 32*(126), 361–366.

Bagley, C., & Pritchard, C. (1998). The reduction of problem behaviours and school exclusion in at-risk youth: An experimental study of school social work with cost-benefit analyses. *Child & Family Social Work, 3*, 219–226.

Barak, A. (2005). Sexual harassment on the Internet. *Social Science Computer Review, 23*(1), 77–92.

Batsche, G., & Knoff, H. (1994). Bullies and their victims: Understanding a pervasive problem in the schools. *School Psychology Review, 23*(2), 165–174.

Beall v. London City School District (No. 2:04-cv-290 (S.D. Ohio, E.D., 2006).

Beaty, L. A., & Alexeyev, E. B. (2008). The problem of school bullies: What the research tells us. *Adolescence, 43*(169), 1.

Black, S. A., & Jackson, E. (2007). Using bullying incident density to evaluate the Olweus Bullying Prevention Programme. *School Psychology International, 28*(5), 623–638.

Bochenek, M., & Brown, A. W. (2001). *Hatred in the hallways: Violence and discrimination against lesbian, gay, bisexual, and transgender students in U.S. schools*. New York: Human Rights Watch.

Bond, L., Carlin, J. B., Thomas, L., Rubin, K., & Patton, G. (2001). Does bullying cause emotional problems? A prospective study of young teenagers. *British Medical Journal, 323*(7311), 480–484.

Borg, M. (1998). Secondary school teachers' perception of pupils' undesirable behaviours. *British Journal of Educational Psychology, 68*(1), 67–79.

Borg, M. (1999). The extent and nature of bullying among primary and secondary schoolchildren. *Educational Research, 41*(2), 137–153.

Bornstein, K. (1998). *My gender workbook*. New York: Routledge.

Boulton, M. J. (1997). Teachers' views on bullying: Definitions, attitudes and ability to cope. *British Journal of Educational Psychology, 67*(Part 2), 223–233.

Boulton, M. J., Bucci, E., & Hawker, D. D. (1999). Swedish and English secondary school pupils' attitudes towards, and conceptions of, bullying: Concurrent links with bully/victim involvement. *Scandinavian Journal of Psychology, 40,* 277–284.

Boulton, M. J., & Flemington, I. (1996). The effects of a short video intervention on secondary school pupils' involvement in definitions of and attitudes towards bullying. *School Psychology International, 17,* 331–345.

Boulton, M. J., Trueman, M., & Flemington, I. (2002). Associations between secondary school pupil's definitions of bullying, attitudes towards bullying, and tendencies to engage bullying: Age and sex differences. *Educational Studies, 23*(4), 353–370.

Brady, K., & Conn, K. (2006, October). Bullying without borders: The rise of cyberbullying in America's schools. *School Business Affairs,* pp. 8–11.

Britzman, D. (2000). Precocious education. In S. Talburt & S. Steinberg (Eds.), *Thinking queer: Sexuality, culture, and education* (pp. 33–60). New York: Peter Lang.

Britzman, D. (2003). *Practice makes practice: A critical study of learning to teach.* Albany: State University of New York Press.

Brown, L. M. (2003). *Girlfighting: Betrayal and rejection among girls.* New York: New York University Press.

Bufkin, J. L. (1999). Bias crime as gendered behavior. *Social Justice, 26*(1), 155–176.

Butler, J. (1990). *Gender trouble.* New York: Routledge Falmer.

California Safe Schools Coalition. (2004). *Consequences of harassment based on actual or perceived sexual orientation and gender non-conformity and steps for making schools safer.* Davis: University of California Press.

Callender, D. R. (2008). When Matt became Jade: Working with a youth who made a gender transition change in high school. In I. Killoran & K. P. Jimenez (Eds.), *Unleashing the unpopular: Talking about sexual orientation and gender diversity in education* (pp. 37–52). Olney, MD: Association for Childhood Education International.

Carr, P. R. (1997). Stuck in the middle? A case study of how principals manage equity-related change in education. *Education Canada, 37*(1), 42–45.

Cartwright, N. (1995). Combating bullying in a secondary school in the United Kingdom. *Journal for a Just and Caring Education, 1*(3), 345–353.

Coggan, C., Bennett, S., Hooper, R., & Dickinson, P. (2003). Association between bullying and mental health status in New Zealand adolescents. *International Journal of Mental Health Promotion, 5*(1), 16–22.

Connell, R. W. (1995). *Masculinities.* Sydney: Allen & Unwin.

Corbett, K., Gentry, C. A., & Pearson, W. J. (1993). Sexual harassment in high school. *Youth & Society, 25*(1), 93–103.

Cowie, H. (1998). Perspectives of teachers and pupils on the experience of peer support against bullying. *Educational Research and Evaluation, 4*(2), 108–125.

Davis v. Monroe County Board of Education (526 U.S. 629 1999).

Dehue, F., Bolman, C., & Vollink, T. (2008). Cyberbullying: Youngsters' experiences and parental perception. *CyberPsychology & Behavior 11*(2), 217–223.

Dignan, J. (2004, January 8). Important victory for gay students. Retrieved October 15, 2007, from http://www.gaycitynews.com/site/index.cfm?newsid=17008546&BRD=2729&PAG=461&dept_id=568864&rfi=8

Dinham, S., Cairney, T., Craigie, D., & Wilson, S. (1995). School climate and leadership: Research into three secondary schools. *Journal of Educational Administration, 33*(4), 36–59.

Doe v. Bellefonte Area School District (3rd Cir. U. S. App. 2004).

Doe v. Brockton Sch. Comm. (No. 2000-J-638 Mass. App. 2000).

Drews v. Joint School District No. 393 (WL 851118 (E.D. Idaho 2006).

Duncan, N. (1999). *Sexual bullying: Gender conflict and pupil culture in secondary schools.* London: Routledge.

Duncan, N. (2004). It's important to be nice, but it's nicer to be important: Girls, popularity and sexual competition. *Sex Education, 4*(2), 137–152.

Duncan, N. (2006). Girls' violence and aggression against other girls: Femininity and bullying in UK schools. In F. Leach & C. Mitchell (Eds.), *Combating gender violence in and around schools* (pp. 51–60). Stoke on Trent, UK: Trentham Books.

Eder, D. (1997). Sexual aggression within the school culture. In B. Bank & P. M. Hall (Eds.), *Gender, equity, and schooling* (pp. 93–112). London: Garland.

Ellis, A. A., & Shute, R. (2007). Teacher responses to bullying in relation to moral orientation and seriousness of bullying. *British Journal of Educational Psychology, 77*(3), 649–663.

Emmett v. Kent School District, 92 F.Supp.2d 1088, 143 Ed. Law Rep. 828 (D.W.D. WA 2000).

Flores v. Morgan Hill. (2004). Agreement re training program and policy changes. Retrieved May 3, 2008, from http://www.nclrights.org/site/DocServer/Flores-Settlement.pdf?docID=641.

Flores v. Morgan Hill Unified School District, No. 02-15128 (9th Cir. 2003).

Franklin v. Gwinett County Public Schools et al. (11th Circuit U.S. Court of Appeals 1992).

Fullan, M. (2000). Leadership for the twenty-first century. In M. Fullan (Ed.), *The Jossey-Bass reader on educational leadership* (pp. 156–163). San Francisco: Jossey-Bass.

Gay and Lesbian Advocates and Defenders. (2000). Brockton court rules in favor of transgender student. Retrieved April 15, 2008, from www.glad.org/Newsroom/press29-10-12-00.shtml

GLSEN. (1999). *National school climate survey.* New York: Author.

GLSEN. (2001). *The national school climate survey: Lesbian, gay, bisexual and transgender youth and their experiences in schools.* New York: Author.

GLSEN & Harris Interactive. (2005). *From teasing to torment: School climate in America, a survey of students and teachers.* New York: Gay, Lesbian and Straight Education Network.

Goldstein, N. (2001). Zero indifference: A how-to guide for ending name-calling in schools. Retrieved January 31, 2004, from www.glsen.org

Gruber, J. E., & Fineran, S. (2008). Comparing the impact of bullying and sexual harassment victimization on the mental and physical health of adolescents. *Sex Roles, 59*, 1–13.

Harris & Associates. (1993). *Hostile hallways: The AAUW survey on sexual harassment in America's schools.* Washington, DC: American Association of University Women.

Harris Interactive. (2001). *Hostile hallways: Bullying, teasing, and sexual harassment in school.* Washington, DC: American Association of University Women Educational Foundation.

Hartsock, N. C. M. (1997). The feminist standpoint. In L. Nicholson (Ed.), *The second wave: A reader in feminist theory* (pp. 216–240). New York and London: Routledge. (Original work published 1993)

Hazler, R. J., Hoover, J. J., & Oliver, R. (1991). Student perception of victimization by bullies in school. *Journal of Humanistic Education and Development, 29*, 143–150.

Henkle v. Gregory, 150 F. Supp. 2d 1067 (Nev. Dist. 2001).

Hinduja, S., & Patchin, J. W. (2008). Cyberbullying: An exploratory analysis of factors related to offending and victimization. *Deviant Behavior, 29*(2), 129–156.

Hoover, J. H., & Juul, K. (1993). Bullying in Europe and the United States. *Journal of Emotional and Behavioral Problems, 2*(1), 25–29.

Irving, B. A., & Parker-Jenkins, M. (1995). Tackling truancy: An examination of persistent non-attendance amongst disaffected school pupils and positive support strategies. *Cambridge Journal of Education, 25*(2), 225–235.

Jaworski, A., & Coupland, N. (1999). Introduction: Perspectives on discourse analysis. In A. Jaworski & N. Coupland (Eds.), *The discourse reader* (pp. 1–44). London: Routledge.

Jenkins, H., & Boyd, D. (2006). Discussion: MySpace and Deleting Online Predators Act (DOPA). *Digital Divide Network.* Retrieved May 31, 2006 from www.digitaldivide.net/articles.

Jones, G. H. (2005, April). *Site-based voices: Dilemmas of educators who engage in activism against student-to-student sexual harassment.* Paper presented at the American Educational Research Association, Montreal, Quebec.

J.S. v. Bethlehem Area School District, 807 A.2d 847 (Pa. 2002).

Katz, J. (Writer). (2002). Tough guise: Violence, media, and the crisis in masculinity. Northhampton, MA: Media Education Foundation.

Kosciw, J. (2004). *The 2003 national school climate survey: The school-related experiences of our nation's lesbian, gay, bisexual and transgender youth.* New York: The Gay, Lesbian and Straight Education Network.

Kosciw, J., & Diaz, E. (2006). *The 2005 national school climate survey: The experiences of lesbian, gay, bisexual and transgender youth in our nation's schools.* New York: Gay, Lesbian, and Straight Education Network.

Lambda Legal. (2001). *Summary of the policy changes adopted as a result of the settlement in Henkle v. Gregory.* New York: Author.

Land, D. (2003). Teasing apart secondary students' conceptualizations of peer teasing, bullying and sexual harassment. *School Psychology International, 24*(2), 147–165.

Larkin, J. (1994). Walking through walls: The sexual harassment of high school girls. *Gender and Education, 6*(3), 263–280.

Layshock v. Hermitage School District, No. 06-116 (W.D. Penn. July 10, 2007).

Lee, V., Croninger, R. G., Linn, E., & Chen, Z. (1996). The culture of sexual harassment in secondary schools. *American Educational Research Journal, 33*(2), 383–417.

Li, Q. (2006). Cyberbullying in schools: A research of gender differences. *School Psychology International, 27*(2), 157–170.

Lincoln, Y. S., & Guba, E. G. (1985). *Naturalistic inquiry.* Beverly Hills, CA: Sage Publications.

Lipkin, A. (1999). *Understanding homosexuality, changing schools.* Boulder, CO: Westview Press.

Macgillivray, I. K. (2004). *Sexual orientation and school policy: A practical guide for teachers, administrators, and community activists.* Oxford: Rowman Littlefield.

Macgillivray, I. K. (2007). *Gay–straight alliances: A handbook for students, educators, and parents.* New York: Harrington Park Press.

Martino, W. (1995). 'Cool boys', 'party animals', 'squids' and 'poofters': Interrogating the dynamics and politics of adolescent masculinities in school. *British Journal of Sociology of Education, 22*(2), 239–263.

Martino, W., & Berrill, D. (2003). Boys, schooling and masculinities: Interrogating the 'right' way to educate boys. *Educational Review, 55*(2), 99–117.

Martino, W., & Pallotta-Chiarolli, M. (2003). *So what's a boy? Addressing issues of masculinity and schooling.* Buckingham, UK: Open University Press.

Mayer, G. R. (1995). Preventing antisocial behavior in the schools. *Journal of Applied Behavior Analysis, 28*(4), 467–478.

Maykut, P., & Morehouse, R. (1994). *Beginning qualitative research: A philosophic and practical guide.* Philadelphia: Routledge.

McIntosh, P. (2004). White privilege and male privilege: A personal account of coming to see correspondence through work in women's studies. In J. F. Healey & E. O'Brien (Eds.), *Race, ethnicity, and gender* (pp. 295–301). London: Pine Forge Press. (Original work published 1988)

Merrell, K. W., Gueldner, B. A., Ross, S. W., & Isava, D. M. (2008). How effective are school bullying intervention programs? A meta-analysis of intervention research. *School Psychology Quarterly, 23*(1), 26–42.

Meyer, E. (2006). Gendered harassment in North America: School-based interventions for reducing homophobia and heterosexism. In C. Mitchell & F. Leach (Eds.), *Combating gender violence in and around schools* (pp. 43–50). Stoke on Trent, UK: Trentham Books

Meyer, E. (2007). "But I'm not gay": What straight teachers need to know about queer theory. In N. Rodriguez & W. F. Pinar (Eds.), *Queering straight teachers* (pp. 1–17). New York: Peter Lang.

Meyer, E. (2008a). A feminist reframing of bullying and harassment: Transforming schools through critical pedagogy. *McGill Journal of Education, 43*(1), 33-48.

Meyer, E. (2008b). Gendered harassment in secondary schools: Understanding teachers' (non)interventions. *Gender & Education, 20*(6), 555–572.

Meyer, E. (2008c). *Policy in practice: How teachers understand and apply school policies in cases of bullying and harassment.* Paper presented at the annual meeting of the American Educational Research Association, New York, NY.

Meyer, E. (in press). Who we are matters: Exploring teacher identities through found poetry. *LEARNing Landscapes*. http://www.learnquebec.ca/en/content/learninglandscapes/

Montgomery v. Independent School District, No. 709, 109 F. Supp. 2d 1081, 1092 (D. Minn. 2000).

Mynard, H., & Stephen, J. (2000). Development of the multidimensional peer-victimization scale. *Aggressive Behavior, 26*(2), 169–178.

Nabozny v. Podlesny, 92 F. 3d 446 (7th Cir. 1996).

National Mental Health Association. (2002). *"What does gay mean?" Teen survey executive summary*. Alexandria, VA: Author.

Naylor, P., & Cowie, H. (1999). The effectiveness of peer support systems in challenging school bullying: The perspectives and experiences of teachers and pupils. *Journal of Adolescence, 22*, 467–479.

Naylor, P., Cowie, H., & del Rey, R. (2001). Coping strategies of secondary school children in response to being bullied. *Child Psychology and Psychiatry Review, 6*(3), 114–120.

Nolin, M. J., Davies, E., & Chandler, K. (1996). Student victimization at school. *The Journal of School Health, 66*(6), 216–221.

O'Conor, A. (1995). Who gets called queer in school? Lesbian, gay, and bisexual teenagers, homophobia, and high school. In G. Unks (Ed.), *The gay teen: Educational practice and theory for lesbian, gay, and bisexual adolescents* (pp. 95–104). New York: Routledge.

Office for Civil Rights. (1997). *Sexual harassment guidance: Harassment of students by school employees, other students or third parties*. Retrieved April 19, 2008, from http://www.ed.gov/about/offices/list/ocr/docs/sexhar01.html

Olweus, D. (1978). *Aggression in the schools: Bullies and whipping boys*. Washington, DC: Hemisphere.

Olweus, D. (1993). *Bullying at school: What we know and what we can do*. Oxford: Blackwell.

Olweus, D. (1996). Bullying at school: Knowledge base and an effective intervention program. *Understanding Aggressive Behavior in Children: Annals of the New York Academy of Sciences, 794*, 265–276.

Olweus, D. (2003). A profile of bullying at school. *Educational Leadership, 60*(6), 12.

Ormerod, A. J., Collinsworth, L. L., & Perry, L. A. (2008). Critical climate: Relations among sexual harassment, climate, and outcomes for high school girls and boys. *Psychology of Women Quarterly, 32*(2), 113–125.

Patton, M. Q. (2002). *Qualitative research and evaluation methods*. Thousand Oaks, CA: Sage.

Pelligrini, A. D., & Long, J. D. (2002). A longitudinal study of bullying, dominance, and victimization during the transition from primary school through secondary school. *British Journal of Developmental Psychology, 20*(2), 259–280.

Perrotti, J., & Westheimer, K. (2001). *When the drama club is not enough: Lessons from the Safe Schools Program for Gay and Lesbian Students*. Boston: Beacon Press.

Phoenix, A., Frosh, S., & Pattman, R. (2003). Producing contradictory masculine subject positions: Narratives of threat, homophobia and bullying in 11–14 year old boys. *Journal of Social Issues, 59*(1), 179–195.

Price, S., & Jones, R. A. (2001). Reflections on anti-bullying peer counselling in a comprehensive school. *Educational Psychology in Practice, 17*(1), 35–40.

Ray v. Antioch Unified School District, 107 F. Supp. 2d 1165 (N.D. Cal. 2000).

Reis, B. (1995). *Safe Schools Anti-Violence Documentation Project: Second annual report.* Seattle, WA: Safe Schools Coalition of Washington.

Reis, B. (1999). *They don't even know me: Understanding anti-gay harassment and violence in schools.* Seattle: Safe Schools Coalition of Washington.

Reis, B., & Saewyc, E. (1999). *83,000 Youth: Selected findings of eight population-based studies.* Seattle: Safe Schools Coalition of Washington.

Renold, E. (2002). Presumed innocence—(Hetero)sexual, heterosexist and homophobic harassment among primary school girls and boys. *Childhood—A Global Journal of Child Research, 9*(4), 415–434.

Renold, E. (2003). 'If you don't kiss me you're dumped': Boys, boyfriends and heterosexualised masculinities in the primary school. *Educational Review, 55*(2), 179–194.

Rich, A. (1993). Compulsory heterosexuality and lesbian existence. In H. Abelove, D. Halperin, & M. A. Barale (Eds.), *The lesbian and gay studies reader* (pp. 227–254). New York: Routledge. (Original work published 1978)

Riehl, C. J. (2000). The principal's role in creating inclusive schools for diverse students: A review of normative, empirical, and critical literature on the practice of educational administration. *Review of Educational Research, 70*(1), 55–81.

Rigby, K., & Cox, I. (1996). The contribution of bullying at school and low self-esteem to acts of delinquency among Australian teenagers. *Personality & Individual Differences, 21*(4), 609–612.

Rigby, K., Cox, I., & Black, G. (1997). Cooperativeness and bully/victim problems among Australian schoolchildren. *Journal of Social Psychology, 137*(3), 357–368.

Rigby, K., & Slee, P. (1999). Suicidal ideation among adolescent school children, involvement in bully-victim problems, and perceived social support. *Suicide and Life-Threatening Behavior, 29*(2), 119–130.

Robinson, K. H. (2005). Reinforcing hegemonic masculinities through sexual harassment: Issues of identity, power and popularity in secondary schools. *Gender and Education, 17*(1), 19–37.

Rofes, E. (1995). Making our schools safe for sissies. In G. Unks (Ed.), *The gay teen: Educational practice and theory for lesbian, gay, and bisexual adolescents* (pp. 79–84). New York: Routledge.

Rollini, G. (2003). *Davis v. Monroe County Board of Education*: A hollow victory for student victims of peer sexual harassment. *Florida State University Law Review, 30,* 987–1014.

Romer v. Evans (517 U.S. 620 1996).

Roth, S. (1994). Sex discrimination 101: Developing a Title IX analysis for sexual harassment in education. *Journal of Law & Education, 23*(4), 459–521.

Ryan, J. (2003). Educational administrators' perceptions of racism in diverse school contexts. *Race, Ethnicity and Education, 6*(2), 145–164.

Salmon, G., & West, A. (2000). Physical and mental health issues related to bullying in schools. *Current Opinion in Psychiatry, 13*(4), 375–380.

Sarkar, M., & Lavoie, C. (2006). *Politique interculturelles et pratiques scolaires en milieu ethnique Montréalais: Apprendre sur le tas?* Paper presented at the Canadian Association for the Practical Study of Law in Education, Montreal, QC.

Schafer, M., Korn, S., Smith, P. K., Hunter, S. C., Mora-Merchan, J. A., Singer, M. M., et al. (2004). Lonely in the crowd: Recollections of bullying. *British Journal of Developmental Psychology, 22*, 379–394.

School District No. 44 (North Vancouver) v. Jubran, 2005 BCCA 201 (BCSC 6 2005).

Seidman, I. (1998). *Interviewing as qualitative research: A guide for researchers in education and the social sciences.* New York: Teacher's College Press.

Shariff, S., & Gouin, R. (2006). Cyber-hierarchies: A new arsenal of weapons for gendered violence in schools. In C. Mitchell & F. Leach (Eds.), *Combating gender violence in and around schools* (pp. 33–42). Stoke on Trent, UK: Trentham Books.

Sharp, S. (1995). How much does bullying hurt? The effects of bullying on the personal well-being and educational progress of secondary aged students. *Educational & Child Psychology, 12*(2), 81–88.

Sharp, S., & Smith, P. K. (1991). Bullying in UK schools: The DES Sheffield Bullying Project. *Early Child Development and Care, 77*, 47–55.

Siann, G., Callaghan, M., Glissove, P., Lockhart, R., & Rawson, L. (1994). Who gets bullied? The effect of school, gender, and ethnic group. *Educational Research, 36*(2), 123–134.

Simmons, R. (2002). *Odd girl out: The hidden culture of aggression in girls.* New York: Harcourt.

Skowronski, S. (2008, April 3). *First amendment rights and sexual orientation harassment in schools.* Paper presented at the annual meeting of the MPSA Annual National Conference, Chicago, IL.

Slee, P. (1995). Bullying: Health concerns of Australian secondary school students. *International Journal of Adolescence & Youth, 5*(4), 215–224.

Smith, G. W. (Ed.) (with D. Smith). (1998). The ideology of "fag": The school experience of gay students. *Sociological Quarterly, 39*(2), 309–335.

Smith, P. K., Mahdavi, J., Carvalho, M., Fisher, S., Russell, S., & Tippett, N. (2008). Cyberbullying: Its nature and impact in secondary school pupils. *Journal of Child Psychology and Psychiatry, 49*(4), 376–385.

Smith, P. K., Smith, C., Osborn, R., & Samara, M. (2008). A content analysis of school anti-bullying policies: Progress and limitations. *Educational Psychology in Practice, 24*(1), 1–12.

Soutter, A., & McKenzie, A. (2000). The use and effects of anti-bullying and anti-harassment policies in Australian schools. *School Psychology International, 21*(1), 96–105.

Stader, D. (2007). *Law and ethics in educational leadership.* Upper Saddle River, NJ: Pearson Education.

Stader, D., & Graca, T. J. (2006, April). *Sexual minority youth and school culture: A study of educational leadership candidates' perceptions of Dallas–Fort Worth area secondary schools.* Paper presented at the American Educational Research Association, San Francisco, CA.

Stein, N. (1995). Sexual harassment in school: The public performance of gendered violence. *Harvard Educational Review, 65*(2), 145–162.

Stein, N. (2002). Bullying as sexual harassment in elementary schools. In E. Rassen (Ed.), *The Jossey-Bass reader on gender in education* (pp. 409–429). San Francisco: Jossey-Bass.

Stein, N., Linn, E., & Young, J. (1992). Bitter lessons for all: Sexual harassment in schools. In J. T. Sears (Ed.), *Sexuality and the curriculum* (pp. 149–174). New York: Teachers College Press.

Stoudt, B. G. (2006). "You're either in or you're out": School violence, peer discipline, and the (re)production of hegemonic masculinity. *Men and Masculinities, 8*(3), 273-287.

Student may sue school for failing to prevent sexual harassment. (2003, April). *Law Reporter,* n.a.

Szlacha, L. (2003). Safer sexual diversity climates: Lessons learned from an evaluation of Massachusetts Safe Schools Program for Gay and Lesbian Students. *American Journal of Education, 110*(1), 58–88.

Theno v. Tonganoxie Unified School District, No. 464 2005 WL 3434016 (D. Kan. 2005).

Timmerman, G. (2003). Sexual harassment of adolescents perpetrated by teachers and peers: An exploration of the dynamics of power, culture, and gender in secondary schools. *Sex Roles, 48*(5–6), 231–244.

Tinker v. Des Moines Independent School District (393 US 503, 509 1969).

Trowbridge, C. (2005, December 29). Former student, district settle lawsuit. *The Tonganoxie Mirror.* Retrieved March 16, 2006, from www.tonganoxiemirror.com

Valdez, F. (2002). Outsider scholars, critical race theory, and "outcrit" perspectivity: Postsubordination vision as jurisprudential method. In F. Valdez, J. M. Culp, & A. P. Harris (Eds.), *Crossroads, directions, and a new critical race theory* (pp. 399–409). Philadelphia: Temple University Press.

Van Manen, M. (1997). *Human science for an action sensitive pedagogy.* London, Ontario: Althouse Press.

Walton, G. (2004). Bullying and homophobia in Canadian schools: The politics of policies, programs, and educational leadership. *Journal of Gay and Lesbian Issues in Education, 1*(4), 23–36.

Warner, M. (1991). Introduction: Fear of a queer planet. *Social Text* (29), 3–17.

Whitley, B. E., Jr. (2001). Gender-role variables and attitudes toward homosexuality. *Sex Roles, 45*(11/12), 691–721.

Williams, T., Connolly, J., Pepler, D., & Craig, W. (2003). Questioning and sexual minority adolescents: High school experiences of bullying, sexual harassment and physical abuse. *Canadian Journal of Community Mental Health, 22*(2), 47–58.

Williams, T., Connolly, J., Pepler, D., & Craig, W. (2005). Peer victimization, social support, and psychosocial adjustment of sexual minority adolescents. *Journal of Youth and Adolescence, 34*(5), 471–482.

Wolak, J., Mitchell, K., & Finkelhor, D. (2006). *Online victimization of youth: Five years later.* Durham, NH: The Crimes against Children Research Center, University of New Hampshire.

Wood, J. (1987). Groping towards sexism: Boys' sex talk. In M. Arnot & G. Weiner (Eds.), *Gender under scrutiny: New inquiries in education* (pp. 187–230). London: Hutchinson Education.

Young, I. M. (1990). *Justice and the politics of difference.* Princeton, NJ: Princeton University Press

Index

About the Author

Elizabeth J. Meyer has been a classroom teacher, outdoor educator, and a Fulbright Teacher Exchange Program grantee. She has been involved in grassroots education and equity work in the United States and Canada for the past 15 years. She completed her M.A. at the University of Colorado, Boulder, and her Ph.D. in education at McGill University in 2007. Meyer has worked as an independent consultant, a researcher, and is an instructor at Concordia and McGill Universities in Montreal, Quebec. Her work has been published in journals such as *Gender and Education, McGill Journal of Education, LEARNing Landscapes,* and *The Journal of GLBT Youth.* She also has written chapters for several books, including *Combating Gender Violence in and Around Schools* (Leach & Mitchell, Eds., 2006), *Media Literacy: A Reader* (Macedo & Steinberg, Eds., 2007), *Queering Straight Teachers* (Rodriguez & Pinar, Eds., 2007), *Girl Culture: An Encyclopedia* (Mitchell & Reid-Walsh, Eds., 2008), *Rocking Your World* (Churchill, Ed., 2009), and *Diversity and Multiculturalism: A Reader* (Steinberg, Ed., 2009).